FAMILY AND CLASS IN A LONDON SUBURB

Reports of
The Institute of Community Studies

★

FAMILY AND CLASS
IN A LONDON SUBURB

★

Peter Willmott
and
Michael Young

LONDON
ROUTLEDGE & KEGAN PAUL

First published 1960
by Routledge & Kegan Paul Ltd
Broadway House, 68–74 Carter Lane
*London, E.C.*4

Printed in Great Britain
by W. & J. Mackay & Co. Ltd, Chatham

People interviewed in this survey have been given
fictitious names and other details about them have
been changed in order to conceal their identities. The
names of roads have also been altered.

CONTENTS

CONTENTS

INTRODUCTION

BETHNAL GREEN and Woodford have never been compared before, and, unless we can persuade other sociologists with different prejudices to repeat our journey across the Hackney Marshes, they probably never will be again. We should explain how they came to be joined. In gathering material for a series of three books on Bethnal Green,[1] we discovered a village in the middle of London. Established residents claimed to 'know everyone'. They could do so because most people were connected by kinship ties to a network of other families, and through them to a host of friends and acquaintances. Ties of blood and marriage were local ties. When they got married, couples did not usually move more than a few steps to set up a new home. They remained close to their parents, close to their brothers and sisters and close to the street markets near which they had been 'bred and born'.

This was rather different from a popular view of what a modern metropolis is like. Bethnal Green is not so much a crowd of individuals—restless, lonely, rootless—as an orderly community based on family and neighbourhood groupings. There is some evidence that the same style of life exists elsewhere in Britain.[2] But the other areas that have been studied are in one important respect like Bethnal Green. They are peopled almost exclusively by manual workers and their families—in other words, they are 'working-class' districts.

[1] Young, M., and Willmott, P., *Family and Kinship in East London;* Townsend, P., *The Family Life of Old People;* Marris, P., *Widows and Their Families.* A full list of books referred to is given in Appendix 6.
[2] Firth, R., *Two Studies of Kinship in London;* Mogey, J. M., *Family and Neighbourhood;* Dennis, N., Henriques, F., Slaughter, C., *Coal is our Life;* Kerr, M., *The People of Ship Street.*

An obvious question to ask is whether this pattern of family and community life is peculiar to the working class—and in cities to the older central areas. Our own small investigation at 'Greenleigh', a new Council estate on the outskirts of London (reported in *Family and Kinship in East London*), had suggested that this might be so. We found people cut off from relatives, suspicious of their neighbours, lonely; the atmosphere very different from the warmth and friendliness of Bethnal Green. But Greenleigh, though a suburb, was still predominantly working class, as well as newly-settled. To be able to make a comparison between social classes we needed a different sort of area altogether. We scanned the 1951 Census Reports in search of a London suburb with a high proportion of middle-class people, and picked the borough, formed by amalgamation, of Wanstead and Woodford. We shall call it Woodford throughout this book.

The question we wanted to answer was whether such a district would have a different kind of family and community life. With the greater mobility their jobs demand, would middle-class people be more isolated from their relatives? Would they be more anxious about status, less sociable with their neighbours? They would, if one believes most of what has been written about suburbs. Novelists have conveyed this impression from H. G. Wells in 1909, whose emancipated *Ann Veronica* escaped from 'Morningside Park' with its 'little red-and-white villas' to the enlightenment of South Kensington; through the Orwell of 1939, who in *Coming Up for Air* described 'Ellesmere Road' on a suburban estate as 'prison with the cells all in a row. A line of semi-detached torture chambers where the poor little five-to-ten-pound-a-weekers quake and shiver'; to Penelope Mortimer in 1958, who set *Daddy's Gone A-Hunting* in a far-out suburb where 'friendships, appearing frank and sunny, were febrile and short-lived, turning quickly to malice.' Lewis Mumford said that the suburb 'lacked the necessary elements for extensive social co-operation, for creative intercourse',[1] F. J. Osborn that it

[1] Mumford, L., *Culture of Cities*, p. 217.

was 'disadvantageous socially. . . . Local community life has been weakened or destroyed.'[1]

No previous sociological studies have been made before in British suburbs, except for municipal housing estates, and in this book we can make only a very partial assessment. Partial, because Woodford is only one suburb, and we do not know how far our findings apply to others. Partial, too, because of prejudice in our informants and in ourselves, which may have led them to give us incorrect answers and us to interpret them wrongly. All that we can say is that we did our best to reduce inaccuracy. We put questions as unambiguous as we could make them to carefully selected samples of Woodford residents, and used appropriate statistical procedures in analysing the results.[2] As a result we are able, on certain subjects and within calculable margins of error, to generalize about the whole population from which our samples were drawn. The 939 members of the general sample described below are in this way a guide to Woodford's total population of 61,000 or so. When, for example, we find that 45% of them belong to clubs or other organizations, we can be fairly sure that if we conducted a census of the whole 61,000, the proportions would not be much different.

The main sources of our information were the interview samples, which were as follows:

1. *The Woodford general sample.* This was a random sample of adults of all ages in Woodford, drawn from the electoral register. Altogether 939 people were interviewed by a small team in the spring of 1959. This sample is the basis of most of the tables in the book, the old age sample being employed for figures, if at all, only on topics which were not asked about in the general survey. The questions put to people in the general sample are reproduced in Appendix 2, and further details about all three samples and the methods of selecting them are in Appendix 1.

[1] Osborn, F. J., Preface to Howard, E., *Garden Cities of Tomorrow*, p. 15.
[2] See Appendix 5, *Tests of Statistical Significance*.

2. *The Woodford marriage sample*. This small sample was chosen for more intensive interview in the autumn of 1959. It consisted of 44 married people with two or more children under 15. Their names were taken, again at random, from people of this kind in the general sample. Most of them were in their thirties; 23 were men, 21 women.

3. *The Woodford old age sample*. This was a random sample of 210 people of pensionable age, that is 65 and over for men, 60 and over for women, picked from the lists of Woodford doctors. This sample was actually interviewed first, in the summer and autumn of 1957. We went on to do more interviewing in Woodford, partly to provide bigger numbers to test the ideas suggested by these first interviews, partly to help produce a fuller account of the suburb, including young people as well as old.

The quotations in the text come from what was said to us by people either in the marriage sample or the old age sample. All informants have been given fictitious names and other details about them have been changed in order to conceal their identities. The names of roads have also been altered. We have depended mainly but not entirely on the interviews. We also tried to keep our eyes open during the three years we spent on the inquiry, and observed as much of interest as we could about Woodford people in public places like streets, shops and trains. We were very fortunate in having in Enid Mills a colleague who lived in the district before and during the period of the inquiry; her knowledge helped us a great deal.

*   *   *

In subsequent chapters the main comparison is with Bethnal Green—how far and in what ways is Woodford different? We are able to compare with three samples from our Bethnal Green inquiries that match those listed above—a Bethnal Green general sample of 933 people drawn from the electoral register, a marriage sample of 45, and an old age sample of 203. But our work in Bethnal Green was done mainly in 1955 and 1956, our work in Woodford in 1957 and 1959. Bethnal Green is changing fast, perhaps even faster than Woodford, and may be growing more like the suburb every day. We ask the reader to remember that when we talk about Bethnal Green, even in the present tense, we are thinking mainly of the place as it was in 1956.

The comparison between the two districts was not our only concern. We also wanted to examine the influence of social class inside Woodford. To do this we had to determine which classes our informants belonged to. There are many possible criteria of social class—family connexions, education, occupation, accent, income, power, property. They are often related to each other—the well-educated man, for instance, is often a well-off man with some property and a professional occupation. But our society is fluid enough so that these attributes are not necessarily matched. The teacher may be well-educated and poor, the director rich and not so well-educated. This means that no single index is entirely satisfactory, though some are better than others. We have adopted occupation, classifying men and single women according to their own job, married women and widows by their husbands'. In a later chapter we introduce two other criteria—the class people themselves *say* they belong to, and where they live in Woodford—but otherwise occupation is the basis of classification used throughout this book. In this, we are following the Registrar General and most other social investigators in this country, who continue to use occupation largely because so many other phenomena, especially of health, have been shown to be correlated with it.[1]

We have divided our informants into two social classes—manual and non-manual, or 'working' and 'middle'. This involved distinguishing in the Registrar General's Class III between manual and non-manual occupations.[2] There were two arguments for making the simple two-fold division. One

---

[1] See Morris, J. N., and Heady, J. A., 'Social and Biological Factors in Infant Mortality', p. 347. Also Glass, D. V., Intro. to *Social Mobility in Britain*, pp. 5–6.

[2] See Appendix 3 for our account of how manual and non-manual workers were distinguished.

was that in occupation Woodford is almost entirely without what many people would think of as an 'upper' or 'upper middle' class. Not only are really wealthy people scarce, but there are very few surgeons or architects, stockbrokers or barristers. The professions are represented by people like bank managers, accountants and surveyors, and such company directors as live there work far more often in small (mainly family) concerns than in large public companies. They seemed to us, in the course of interviewing, to have lives not sharply different from those of other white-collar workers—the bank clerks, insurance agents, shopkeepers, civil servants and teachers who appeared so often on the interview schedules.

The second—and more telling—argument was that in dividing our informants into two main social classes we were doing what our informants themselves did. We tried to find out what classes people thought (or perhaps 'felt' would be the better word) existed in Woodford, and the commonest view was that there were two, usually described as 'middle' and 'working' or 'lower'.

The main themes of this book are the differences between the suburb and the East End, and the differences between the middle and working-class residents of Woodford. In Chapter I we describe the suburb in general terms. Chapters II to VII are about family life, Chapter VIII and the following ones about the local community.

*   *   *

The research on which this book is based was supported by grants from the Ford Foundation of New York and, in its later stages, from the Joseph Rowntree Memorial Trust of York. We are grateful to both these bodies and also to the many people who advised us and gave us their comments on various drafts of the report, particularly Professor Richard Titmuss, the Chairman of the Institute, and members of the Institute's Advisory Committee—Dr. John Bowlby, Sir Alexander Carr-Saunders, Dr. Morris Carstairs, Euan

Cooper-Willis, Leonard Elmhirst, William Elmhirst, Geoffrey Gorer, Robin Huws Jones, Professor Charles Madge, J. L. Peterson, Dr. J. H. Sheldon, Professor Edward Shils, Peter Townsend, Lewis Waddilove and William Wallace. In addition we would like to acknowledge the helpful criticism received from Ann Cartwright, Edmund Cooney, David Donnison, Jean Floud, James Hallsmith, Margot Jefferys, Sasha Moorsom, Stephen Shenck, John Sparrow, Paul Stirling and Alan Stuart.

We would also like to thank our colleagues at the Institute. First those who helped us, as well as in many other ways, by interviewing old people, Enid Mills, Peter Marris and Peter Townsend; second, those who helped us by their criticism, Mary Barclay, Howard Dickinson and Ralph Samuel; and third Daphne Chandler and Polly Kasserer who were endlessly patient and efficient in typing interview reports and manuscripts. Phyllis Willmott assisted throughout in the analysis of material and preparation of the draft. William Elmhirst supervised the interviewing for the general survey in conjunction with Cynthia Seabrook. We are indebted to Research Services Ltd. for allowing Miss Seabrook to work with us for a period.

Finally we want to express our gratitude to people in Wanstead and Woodford. The Borough Council and its officers kindly gave their assistance, placing an office at our disposal during a critical period, and a number of local doctors also generously helped us. But above all we owe thanks to the many hundreds of local citizens who generously gave us of their time and knowledge, and particularly to those of our informants who gave valuable further help by writing detailed diaries.

I

PROFILE OF A SUBURB

WHEN we first visited Woodford it was clear that we had come to a different kind of place from Bethnal Green. East End children do not trot their ponies along forest paths wearing velvet hunting caps. East End houses do not have stone gnomes in their back-yards. There are no golf courses near the docks.

How few people there seemed to be in Woodford, and how many dogs! This was perhaps what Orwell was talking about when he wrote of 'the huge peaceful wilderness of outer London . . . sleeping the deep, deep sleep of England.'[1] In Bethnal Green there are noisy people everywhere, large mothers with oilskin shopping bags, young mothers in red high-heeled shoes, children playing around the stalls of the street markets, neighbours talking to each other from one door to another. The suburb is sliced by main roads, and the cars and long-distance buses speeding to Southend and Newmarket leave only a distant hum in hundreds of empty sideroads. In Bethnal Green people are vigorously at home in the streets, their public face much the same as their private. In Woodford people seem to be quieter and more reserved in public, somehow endorsing Mumford's description of suburbs as the apotheosis of 'a collective attempt to lead a private life'.[2]

In Bethnal Green homes and factories are packed tight and surrounded with asphalt, whereas in Woodford the houses are spaced out at intervals and surrounded by grass. 'Traditionally, Woodford has always endeavoured', says the official

[1] Orwell, G., *Homage to Catalonia*, p. 314.
[2] Mumford, L., op. cit., p. 215.

guide-book, 'to keep the disadvantages of civilization at a proper distance without permitting the advantages to escape it.'[1] The disadvantage of civilization is evidently industry, while the advantages are the cultivated trees and flowers, the garages and the Tudor half-timbering which a modern economy makes possible. The most important physical difference is that there is relatively much more space—in 1959 Woodford had 61,000 people upon 3,842 acres, a density of 16 per acre, while Bethnal Green's 49,000 people were pressed in on 760 acres, at a density of 64 to each acre.

Woodford comes from Bethnal Green

The contrast is all the more striking because Woodford and Bethnal Green both belong to East London.[2] Although Woodford is officially in Essex, there is no visible boundary between it and London. Buildings stretch almost all the way from Bethnal Green through Leyton to Woodford, and now even farther out to the belt of new Council estates.

This unity is more than geographical. The suburbs grew out from the city, where most of their inhabitants came from. The population of Woodford has been rising rapidly all this century, most sharply of all in the boom years of private building immediately before the war—the annual rate of increase was 1,600 in the 'thirties, as compared with 660 in the 'twenties and 810 between 1946 and 1951. A few of the additional people have come from rural Essex and East Anglia. Many of the countrymen came off the land to be gardeners, the country-women to be servants in the big houses around Epping Forest. Mrs. Arrell had come from East Anglia, where her father was a farmer.

'I was brought up on a farm,' she said, 'We had all the fruit and vegetables you could want. There was an orchard with Blenheim

---

[1] *Wanstead and Woodford Official Guide*, p. 43.
[2] One authority includes the following in 'East London'—Stepney, Poplar, Bethnal Green, Hackney, Shoreditch in the County of London; and West Ham, East Ham, Walthamstow, Leyton, Wanstead and Woodford, Ilford, Barking and Dagenham in the County of Essex: Sinclair, R., *East London*, p. 32.

apples for eating, pears and strawberries. I remember we used to go often to Felixstowe for the day. Father would pick a great load of vegetables and fruit, and put it in the baskets. Then he'd take us down to the station, set us in the carriage and put the baskets on our laps. We used to love the scenery, with all the little rabbits bobbing out to look at the train. All my brothers and sisters are fond of gardening like me. It was born in us.'

These people of 'good farming stock', as one of them put it, met in Woodford the far greater flood coming in the other direction from the city.[1] Fifteen per cent of all the people living in Woodford (as represented by our general sample) were born in the East End, 26% in the inner Essex boroughs of Leyton, East Ham, West Ham and Walthamstow, and 20% elsewhere in Greater London.[2] The rest, apart from the 12% born in Woodford itself, came from the provinces, where more younger people originated than older —29% of the 414 people in their thirties and forties were born outside Greater London, against 18% of the 90 people aged 70 or over. But people from the inner London districts are still the core of suburban society. Often they have arrived by stages, they or their parents moving, as children or after marriage, from Bethnal Green or Poplar to Walthamstow or Forest Gate, and then on to Woodford. Their starting point is impressed on them all the same.

The move outwards is also a move upwards. When Mr. Lloyd said, with understandable pride, that he had come a long way, he was not thinking of miles. An engineering foreman, he is an example of a man, born in Shadwell, who now owns a six-roomed Edwardian house, red brick with white gate, tiled porch and glass-panelled front door, in a quiet leafy road at Wanstead.

---

[1] The movement of population to the eastern outskirts of London from both directions—out from the East End and in from rural Essex and other counties—has been noted before. See Smith, H. L., 'Influx of Population', pp. 61–66.

[2] 'Greater London' is as defined by the Census, 1951. See e.g. *Occupation Tables*, pp. xiii–xiv. 'East End' is the boroughs of Stepney, Poplar, Bethnal Green, Hackney and Shoreditch.

'I've come quite a long way', he told us, 'from being a Shadwell boy earning 5s a week to having my own house out here.' At 28 he had married a girl from Hackney and to begin with they lived in two rooms at Bow. 'The house came up for sale after a couple of years', he explained, 'and I tried to buy it. But I couldn't afford it. After that, I said to the wife, "I'm going to work hellish hard the next five years. You help me and I promise you you'll have your own house." And I did it. Six years later I paid the deposit on a small house at Leytonstone. We couldn't afford to furnish the whole house at first, so we let off half of it, but it was a footing, a foundation, something I could build on.' By 1936 he had enough money to pay the deposit on his present house. 'It's a good feeling', he said, 'the feeling that you've achieved something. Something you've done. Something you're proud of. I could have stayed in the East End, but it didn't appeal to me. I wanted something better for my family. There's always something better than what you've got if only you're prepared to work for it.'

If social class has an edge in Woodford, it is partly because so many of its people come from the East End. 'We don't tell people we come from Bethnal Green,' said one woman, 'You get the scum of the earth there.' Mr. Barber said, 'The East End is a different class altogether—people there call you Dad or Uncle or Auntie. We don't get any of that here.' Another man said:

'Half the people round here are from the East End. I came from Bow to East Ham. Then I moved out here so my children had somewhere to play. The forest was nice for them. The road where I was in Bow as a boy all did the same sort of thing. It was on account of the Jews. It was all Jews coming in and English moving out.'

Although people talk about travelling 'up to town', in this social context 'out' means 'up', up the 'ladder', up 'in the social scale', up 'in the world'. It was as though, in the mind's eye, people had turned the whole of East London on its side like a geological exhibit in a giant-sized museum. There deep down in the lowest strata were Bethnal Green and Step-

4

ney and there at the top Woodford and Wanstead. To clamber up the slope was success, to remain at the bottom, failure. Once you had clambered up you wanted to be distinguished as clearly as possible from those who had given up or never tried. This was one reason why people wanted a change in the postal address. Half of the borough was in the same London postal district as the East End. The demand was that the whole should henceforth be known as Essex instead. 'We're under Essex for cricket—when there's a match in Woodford it's the Essex County team—so why shouldn't we be for the post office?'

Woodford is no haven: it suffers from the dynamic disequilibrium which in some degree afflicts nearly all sought-after districts in an open society—more people flock in from East London because the suburb is desirable and by so doing make it less desirable for those who were there before. The older people among our informants were only too well aware that the newcomers constantly detract from the value of the district. One married couple discussed the problem in the course of an interview.

HUSBAND. 'People have got more money than they used to have and are spreading outwards. Consequently we are getting more people from the East End of London. We're not snobs, you know, but they're a different type of person from our type.'
WIFE. 'Of course, people have always been coming out here from the East End of London, you can't complain about that.'
HUSBAND. 'No, but they're a different type. In the old days it was professional people and people like that. Now, the professional people haven't got the money to put down for a house; it's only the working people who can afford to do that. There's no doubt about it, the social aspect of the district has gone down.'

At the time of the evacuation during the war, said one woman, 'there were lots of big houses here to requisition and they brought thousands of homeless East-Enders in. They can't help it but their manners don't improve the place.' 'There was a great difference when East-Enders evacuated,'

5

another man told us, 'they were really common.' Migration has continued since the war and always with the same consequence—'the tone's gone down', or 'the class has gone down', or 'I don't know where they come from but some of them are, well, without being snobby, they seem to me to be just a little bit lower.'

The decline of the gentry

The process is the more painful because the attraction of the low class has led to the repulsion of the high. Every year since anyone can remember some of the most respected citizens of Woodford have been marching northwards after the receding countryside or southwards to a watering place. 'The better class of people', as one man put it, 'are moving further afield.' 'The people with money', said another, 'seem to be going out towards Chigwell. Woodford is getting more mixed.' Some of our informants remembered the 'old days' when 'the gentry', 'the big people', 'the aristocracy' still lived in Woodford—the Henry Fowlers, the Smith-Harrisons, and Sir Albert Spicer and Sir John Roberts. One old lady said, with a nice sense of distinction, 'There were people on the Green then that were nearly County'. Our older informants were full of nostalgic stories.

'When Mummy and I came to live in this house there were only three or four houses here at all. There was a pond down by the railway, and every winter we used to skate on it after they'd tested the ice by driving a horse and wagon on to it. Sir John Roberts and all the big families from round about used to come too and in the middle of the morning the butler would come down from Arnold Hills' place and skate all round the pond with a tray of hot coffee.'

'Every year we were allowed to go in the big house twice—once at the Flower Show and once to see the rhododendrons—oh, they were lovely. Then Sir John used to have wonderful fireworks and we all went there then.'

'When I was a boy I was out with my father one day and he suddenly said, "Take your cap off, boy. Here comes Mr. Smith-

6

Harrison." So when we came up to him, I took my cap off and
my father touched his cap. I said, "Why did we have to do that,
Dad?" He said, very seriously, "Because, my boy, he's the Lord
of the Manor".'

To long-term residents old Woodford seemed to have been
populated by two classes, far removed and therefore easily
distinguishable from each other—wealthy people and working people, gentry and others, big people and little people. If
we were to believe one or two of the residents we saw from
the last category, these were not two nations in strife but two
groups knowing their place and contented with it: 'Years ago
they was all gentry and they treated you as friends.' Mrs.
Strong put it more bluntly:

> 'Jack's as good as his master today. When each of them knew
> their position, the people like the Smith-Harrisons were re-
> spected, they were looked up to and they were happy and other
> people were happy and quite friendly.'

For the Mrs. Strongs, the world would never be so secure
again. They had lost from Woodford 'the old-fashioned
English type of family', and the newcomers were just not so
'genuine' as the original inhabitants.

There is still one aristocrat who retains a connexion with
the district. Sir Winston Churchill has been the local Member
of Parliament since 1924, and many residents claim acquain-
tance with him. Mr. Adams, for instance, explained that he
had had some trouble over the stopper that he was using to do
up the front of his house.

> 'I wrote to Churchill to tell him that I'd helped to push him along
> to Westminster and that it was ridiculous, the stopper was a
> swindle. Churchill said I should write to the Minister of Housing
> so that put them on tension. They pay more attention if I can say
> he told me to write. When I went up to the meeting at the Haw-
> key Hall I clapped him on the back and said "Good old Winnie".'

> 'I suppose he is too old for the job,' said Mrs. Ross during the
> 1959 General Election, 'but he's a dear. When my Alan was a
> baby he pulled up in his car and got out and said "My dear, what

beautiful children". It was the way he said it, he sounded as though he really meant it. Alan liked him, and I think if children like him he must be pretty good.'

'Do you know, he's actually used my fountain pen,' said Mrs. Bolton, an active Conservative. 'He sat in this very room and borrowed my pen during the previous election. It's a wonderful experience to meet a man like that.'

But although Sir Winston is liked by many of his constituents, and has become a legendary figure far beyond Woodford, for many of its long-standing residents he does not make up for the loss of Sir John Roberts.

The vanished villages

As Sir John Roberts and the other 'big families' have died out or moved out, Woodford has become less rural. On the very ground where butlers used once to carry trays of drinks now stand rows of villas. It was different in the days when 'it was a wonder to go to the magic lantern at the Band of Hope' and Woodford was a 'wild, empty, open sort of place'.

'The minute I got off the bus at the hotel I saw that house on the corner there, you know where Smith's motor showrooms is now, with its big iron gates and the lawn and those peacocks walking across the lawn behind those iron gates and that green and the little houses and I thought, "This is the place I've been looking for all my life—a nice country village within easy reach of London".'

'This place was like fairyland when we first came. It was so beautiful before they brought the people in from the slums. In the old days we had four or five titled people around here. I don't know how they can spoil the beauty. They can never put it back.'

'When I was young, all the way up the lane here the hedges were ten feet high and full of may trees, and the fields from here to the Roding were one mass of buttercups. When I made my way up the Green to go to the church I would hear the bells of four or five churches round about. Now the high buildings and the noise of traffic blocks it out and you can't even hear your own church bell.'

All this has given way to something so different that, in the words of one horrified man, Woodford is now 'well, you might say like Leytonstone'.

It would be wrong to suggest that the old Woodford, which many people find so endearing, has altogether lost its character. The names of the districts into which the borough is loosely divided still recall the villages which used to line the main roads of stage-coach times—Snaresbrook, Wanstead, Woodford Wells, Woodford Green, Woodford Bridge. They were joined up by twentieth-century ribbon development. But the greatest survival is the Forest. The Royal Forest of Essex[1] no longer covers great distances of 'woody grounds and fruitful pastures, privileged for wild beasts and fowls of forest chase and warren, to rest and abide there in safe protection of the king for his delight and pleasure.'[2] But its successor, Epping Forest, still stretches green fingers all the way from Wanstead through Lords Bushes, Cuckoo Brook, Deershelter Plain and Ambresbury Banks to Epping; it is entrusted by the City of London to Conservators charged with preserving its natural aspect, its hornbeams and oaks, its nuthatches and owls, for ever. Commoners, that is farmers or other owners or occupiers of at least a half-acre of land in any of the Forest parishes, are still allowed to graze their cattle, horses, sheep and pigs on the Forest, provided they are branded as in the Middle Ages by the Reeve of the parish from which they come. In the final stages of our survey there were still nearly 100 branded cattle loose in the Forest. In that marvellously hot and dry summer of 1959 several Woodford residents complained about some of the cattle which broke through into their gardens to eat carefully watered flowers and bushes. Cars have slaughtered some of

[1] Although all Crown rights were terminated by the Epping Forest Act of 1878 a link with the past is provided by the Crown appointment of the Duke of Gloucester as Forest Ranger. See Qvist, A., *Epping Forest*.
[2] Buxton, E. N., *Epping Forest*, p. 6.

the cattle and some of the black deer also. But the ancient Forest herd still exists, 70-strong, along with such Woodford badgers and foxes, stoats and hares as keep away from the headlights of businessmen hurrying home at night.

In the buildings too there are a few remnants to be seen of the period before 1856 when the railway came to join Woodford to its future. Highams still stands, although now transformed into a County High School. It is near Hurst House on Woodford Green, known affectionately by local people as the *Naked Beauty*. By Johnson's Pond, where carts and coaches were once driven through the water between a row of stakes to wash the dust away, there is a timber house of the type which must have at one time predominated in the villages on the edge of the Forest. But Wanstead House and its great gardens constructed at a time 'when Nature was universally subdued by Art',[1] and with it most of the other fine houses that belonged to the gentry, have been destroyed. From 1856 on Nature has been further subdued by Increase of Population, as one after the other the 'big families' have sold their estates for parcelling up into building plots. Some of the old names have been preserved in the new estates of small houses. People still live, as they will proudly explain, on Monkham's Estate or the Knighton Estate. (The modern use of the old word 'estate' for Council properties has not debased it for these owner-occupiers.) Laing's Estate, named after the firm who built it, is exceptional in having no such link with the past. The process continues, not so much through the sale of estates as of large houses standing, as they say, in their own grounds. These are still being replaced by small and more modern villas, four or six where there used to be one house suited to households of Victorian size.

Each period produces its characteristic houses—the late Victorian, the Edwardian, the inter-war and the post-war. But the more distant past has never been abandoned. Antiquity is always there in the estate agent's advertisements, even for the most modern of houses.

[1] Dunlop, I., and Kimball, F., 'The Gardens of Wanstead House, Essex.'

WOODFORD GREEN
IMPOSING MODERN SEMI-DETACHED PROPERTY
WITH BOLD HALF-TIMBERED FRONTAGE

The elevation is in brick, rough cast and half timber with over-hanging mellowed tiles between the seven Tudor style bay windows.
The accommodation comprises a ground floor SQUARE SEMI-LOUNGE with delf rack and coved ceiling. DINING-ROOM with tiled Claygate fireplace in Mahogany surround. FRONT RECEPTION ROOM with polished tongued and grooved oak flooring and coved ceiling. CHEERFUL WORK-ING KITCHEN in ivory with recently installed 'Ideal' boiler, Butler's sink set fitted with Supa taps, Ascot multipoint heater, double eye level cabinet . . . A MOST DELIGHTFUL ROOM. Separate downstairs toilet with low flush suite in green. NEAT GARDEN with dwarf brick wall, crazy paving, rockeries and integral garden-tool shed. COPPER SERVICE throughout.

In England the new is only acceptable if it embodies the old, and nowhere has this lesson been more fully learnt than in house-design. Each house is a miniature history of architecture. Victorian houses suggest the medieval by their gabled roofs and their oriel-like windows; and recall Athens or Venice through marble pillars with ornate capitals. Archaism is at its more bizarre in the semi-detached, pebble-dashed villas built since 1918 which are more than the symbol, they *are* the suburb. Many have bow windows with leaded panes; many represent half-timbering by creosoted laths nailed to brick fronts; some have front doors encased in Norman arches. The houses privately built after 1945 express the same hankering for the first Elizabeth and for earlier times by stained 'Cathedral' glass which is used for the top halves of doors and in the round windows of halls and lavatories. The post-war houses have the distinction of roofs with uniform tiling but many of the pre-war have tiles half red, half pink where they were replaced after bombing, like a scar that is still visible despite the new skin.

The trees with which Woodford abounds also express its development. The old trees are oaks, elms, hawthorns, chestnuts, limes and sycamores, and those that stand are now protected against further destruction by the Welfare State in the shape of the Tree Warden in the County Planning Department. After 1918 a new phase of planting began. There was a demand in the newly-built street for trees which would give a country air to the place while preserving the tidy appearance proper to a respectable suburb. The Borough Engineer sought to avoid root trouble under pavements and foundations and obstruction to light or traffic from overhead branches; and at the same time to achieve quick growth, hardiness, ease of maintenance. And he chose the flowering cherries (pink rather than white), the crab apples, the almonds, the mountain ashes, purple plums and laburnums which now line hundreds of local streets. Old residents remember how the children once decorated the churches at Easter-time with primroses, wind flowers and dog violets from the Forest and the fields, and twined ivy around the altar rails; now in a more cosmopolitan world Easter is welcomed by magnificent boughs of Siberian quince and Japanese cherry.

So, on the surface at any rate, Woodford was not unsuitable for our purpose. It is different from Bethnal Green in all kinds of ways—in its spaciousness, its flower gardens, its trees, its private schools, its owner-occupied 'desirable residences', its leafy avenues and crescents—and many such differences seem to reflect the class character of the two districts. Any observer would, we think, confirm that Woodford has a 'middle-class' character as surely as Bethnal Green has a 'working-class'.

Woodford working class

This does not mean, of course, that Woodford is peopled exclusively by the middle class. There is not a borough in the country without a sizeable proportion of manual workers— Woodford is no more an exception than Chelsea, Bournemouth or Harrogate. Of the 921 people in the general sample whose occupational class is known, 38% are manual workers or their wives, 62% non-manual.

Some of the manual workers are natives of the place, the children of farmworkers or brickmakers; others came as children with their parents in an earlier decade; others again have moved to buy their own house in Woodford in the past twenty years. And, though some live in semi-detached villas in predominantly middle-class roads, most do not. There are pockets of working-class housing scattered all the way through the district—the Council flats and houses which manage to look the same in every part of England; the faded yellow-brick houses built for the workers in the brickfields at the end of the last century; the cottages built for servants and gardeners, now occupied by mechanics and lorry-drivers; the bigger old houses now converted into three with a common bathroom on the landing.

We saw something of the variety in people's lives as we went about our inverviewing. Our informants sometimes engulfed us in deep, velvet-covered settees, and handed us glasses of sherry which we had to hold gingerly in the left hand while unchivalrously scribbling notes with the right. In another street we were seated on hard upright chairs next to drying nappies and given a large cup of the sweet tea and sterilized milk which we had come to know in Bethnal Green. One house would have thick pile carpets, rooms fashionably decorated with oatmeal paper on three walls and a contrasting blue on the fourth, bookcases full of Charles Dickens, Agatha Christie and *Reader's Digest* condensed books, above the mantelpiece a water-colour of Winchelsea, Vat 69 bottles converted into table-lamps, french windows looking out on to a terra-cotta Pan in the middle of a goldfish pond, the whole bathed in a permanent smell of Mansion polish. Five minutes away a smaller house had peeling paint showing green beneath the cream, rexine-covered sofas polished in the sit-down places like a long-worn pair of trousers, brown linoleum cracked around the edges and, in place of the polish, a faint but equally permanent smell of leaking gas and boiled greens. We encountered neat grey suits, gold watch chains, bow-ties, clipped moustaches and shiny brown shoes; also men collarless and in shirt-sleeves, with waistcoats and over-size carpet slippers. As well as the middle-aged mothers with faces made up and hair colour-rinsed, wearing two-pieces and nylon stockings, there were plump 'Mums' of the same age wearing lisle stockings and enormous flowered overalls. One would tell us she starts her day with grilled kidneys and coffee and ends it with 'buttered cream crackers and cheese and port'; another that she begins with cornflakes and tea and ends with cocoa.

Yet the suburb as a whole certainly bears a middle-class stamp, probably more now than ever before. On their way to work electricians and bank clerks wear the same sort of clothes, and, what is more, so do their wives. They sometimes drive the same sort of cars, and sometimes the interiors of their houses are indistinguishable too. In each you can watch the same television set from the same mass-produced sofa. In the homes of the young couples there are plenty of signs of the post-war redistribution of incomes which can be viewed instead as the general adoption of middle-class standards. In the following pages we shall explore the similarities as well as the differences between the classes.

II

HOUSE-CENTRED COUPLES

THIS book, being about the family, is also about husbands and wives. Most of what we know about Woodford is described through their eyes and ears. As our chief informants, they have portrayed their relationships with other people within their families and without, they have given us a sense of the social world which they see around them. But they have not described themselves, unless inadvertently; they have not told us, except in passing, of their inner life nor of how they view each other, husband, wife, and wife, husband.

Must we then say nothing about this relationship? We wrote down everything that seemed significant—detailed interview reports which allow us to form an impression. When in Bethnal Green we decided that the old picture of husbands and wives, as drawn by Mayhew, Booth and their successors, was no longer true to life. In place of the traditional working-class husband, as mean with his money as he was callous in sex, forcing a trial of unwanted babies upon his wife, has come the man who wheels the pram on Saturday mornings. In Woodford, what has happened? Is it the same story there, of progress towards a more stable domestic partnership?

There are not the same reference points in the past as there were for the East End. Unlike novels, social investigations in England have nearly always been about others, not their authors, and the favourite others have been slum-dwellers, about whom there is a respectable literature. For the working-class East End, comparisons of a sort could therefore be made over time. But to reconstruct the past of middle-class families we have to go outside Woodford. When historical comparisons have been made before, the usual conclusion has been that industrialization has not strengthened but weakened the partnership which is at the centre of the family.

In the agricultural families which predominated until well into the nineteenth century, husbands and wives worked as one. 'At the end of the nineteenth century a good wife was as essential to a farmer's prosperity as she was in the Middle Ages. She played as important a part in the life of the farm community.'[1] There was a division of labour, but it was within the family and between husbands, wives and children. It was the same in the handicraft industries centred in the home which struggled on into the twentieth century. In all but the richest middle-class families, businesses were conducted jointly. But eventually, with the decline of the old, independent middle class, and the rise of large-scale industry, fathers were forced out of the house to get paid jobs if they were to have any income, and economic functions were transferred from the domestic to the wider economy. It is easy to see this as the beginning of a one-way process which has continued without check ever since.

> 'The transfer process', say two eminent sociologists, 'is not yet finished. Men's functions were among the first to leave the homestead as farming was given up. Women's more varied household duties have been transferred more slowly.'[2]

But transferred they have been. Women have bought bread instead of baking it, sent their washing to commercial laundries, and bought clothes instead of making them.

Suburban extreme

One would expect that this process, of removing from the home both men and women's functions, would have gone

[1] Stenton, D. M., *The English Woman in History*, p. 117. See also Young, G. M., *Victorian England*, p. 21.
[2] Ogburn, W. F., and Nimkoff, M. F., *A Handbook of Sociology*, p. 472. See also Burgess, E. W., and Locke, H. J., *The Family: From Institution to Companionship*.

furthest in a dormitory suburb. Home and workplace are certainly separated by distance. Of the 572 people in the general sample who were in paid work, 76% worked outside the borough. Taking London as a whole the *average* time taken from door to door in the journey to work was 42 minutes;[1] in Woodford many people have much longer to go than that.

> 'I have to walk to the station first of all. It takes me altogether an hour and a half to get to work and more to get home at night. They push them into the trains like sardines. I can't even read my evening paper till Leytonstone, there's such a crush.'

What the wife does in Essex and the husband in London are quite different. Here are some extracts taken every three-quarters of an hour or so from the diaries written by a teacher and his wife for a particular Thursday morning in October 1959.

Mr. Matthews	Mrs. Matthews
7.15 a.m.	
Got up reluctantly when the alarm rang. Went downstairs, put the dog out and made a pot of tea, taking a cup up to Doris. Took my own cup of tea into the bathroom, while I washed and shaved. Finished dressing and then downstairs to breakfast.	Frank brought me my usual cup of tea in bed. Got up and went down in my dressing-gown to get his breakfast. Said good morning to our little Sealyham, Dennis—he rolls on his back and waits for me to tickle him.
8 a.m.	
Left the house. A brisk walk to the station as usual—otherwise I would miss the train that goes through Snaresbrook at about 8.10. Bought my *Times* at the station bookstall, where I have one ordered. Read *The Times* on	Frank left for work and Dennis and I walked to the gate to see him off. Waited until Frank had disappeared round the bend in the road, then went indoors and called the children and prepared their breakfast.

[1] *London Travel Survey 1949*, p. 29.

the train and was irritated by being turned out at Leyton-stone to wait for another.

8.45 a.m.

Arrived at school. Collected the classroom key and went to un-lock door. Eastwood and Good, who are monitors, were waiting outside the door as usual. Took my coat to the staff room, and when I got back found that most of the other boys had arrived. Took the register and went up to Assem-bly with the class. The Head announced the times of the Record and Chess Clubs, but as usual no one could hear him.

Got Susan ready for school and took her round there. Then went on to the shops. On the way back saw Mrs. Rayburn, who has been ill with flu—I stopped to ask her how she was feeling.

9.15 a.m.

Returned to classroom for first period. Awaited for arrival of 4C, which takes ten minutes longer than anyone else. We made a start on the trial scene from *The Merchant of Venice*; they seemed to get the general feeling of it well, but will they understand most of the detail when we come to examine it more carefully next week?

Arrived home. Combed Den-nis, then did the bed-making, then started on the dishes. I like to see the bright cheerful colours of the plates emerge from the soapy water. 'House-wives' Choice' on the radio also cheers me up.

10 a.m.

Second Period. I took the Second-year 6th 'A'-level group. Harrington announced that he did not intend to go on to do 'S'-level after all, because his parents couldn't afford any more years at school. I tried to

My friend Joyce called. She wanted to know if I would go over to her house for tea that afternoon, instead of the next day, as previously arranged. I agreed. We started a discussion about washing machines.

dissuade him and the period developed into quite a discussion.

10.45 a.m.

Morning break. I went to the staff room for tea. Talked with Anderson about two boys in my class. He says he caught them fighting quite violently yesterday. This might not matter so much if they were younger, but they are 16. Anderson and I discussed tactics—which made a change from the interminable political discussions we've had lately in the staff room.

Joyce having gone, I took Dennis out for his morning walk in the Forest. We have made a lot of friends on these walks—dog-owners seem to find it very easy to get talking to each other. Saw my friend Shirley out with her Dachshund, Oscar. We stopped for a chat about the party we both were at last Saturday.

Obviously it is not easy for Mr. and Mrs. Matthews to share their interests in the way they would if they ran a farm together. Mrs. Matthews likes to hear about the people her husband works with; she is not thrilled to hear about 'S'-Level candidates, and even if she were once, the excitement would not last long.

Sometimes the split between the lives of husband and wife has been driven so far that they hardly seem to inhabit the same world. We are not thinking so much of the working-class husband who spends most of his time and his money out of Woodford altogether, drinking and gambling.

> 'There's a man in the next street—he's a whisky drinker. He comes back dead drunk after the pubs close at night. Sometimes his children have to go out and pick him up from the street.'

People like this, though rare these days, were already familiar to us in Bethnal Green. They are modern replicas of the absentee husbands of Mayhew's time whose refuge from a miserable and crowded home was the 'conversation, warmth and merriment of the beer-shop, where they can take their ease among their "mates".'[1]

We are thinking rather of a different sort of absentee husband, at the opposite end of the social scale—the executive who spends nearly all his time out of the home not so much spending money as making it. There are many manual workers in Woodford who snatch at every chance of overtime and stay in their factories night after night to earn money for a washing machine, a refrigerator or a small car. (Always it is a *small* car that people talk about as though not even a puritan could object as long as it is not a *large* car they want.) But they do not ordinarily work anything like as long as some of their employers.

Mr. Lane, for instance, manages his own small factory close by. He gets to work every morning at 8 and often doesn't leave for home until 10 or 11 at night. 'I like Woodford,' he said, 'because it's so near the factory. I've got a bar in my office but sometimes I like to bring a business friend back for a drink here. And if I suddenly decide to fly overseas I can dart back in ten minutes and get a bag for the night!' Mr. Milner was of a similar sort. An accountant in a large company, he did not have such long hours in his office but almost every night and every week-end he brought papers back home to work on in his study. He too had to make frequent business trips.

Some men like these work very long hours, spend a good deal of time travelling and do not necessarily share even their leisure with their families—much of it being spent with business colleagues. They may even enjoy (or have to put up with) quite a different standard of living from that at home. Profligate working-class husbands keep most of their earnings (and the knowledge about the size of their pay-packets) strictly to themselves. The high executive, for his part, may also have much larger dinners with his business colleagues

[1] Mayhew, H., *London Labour and the London Poor*, Vol. I, p. 11.

than he ever does with his wife and children at home, and live in luxury when he makes trips abroad.[1]

The past revived

In so far as a few executives seem most at home when they are at work, their families are the opposite of those nineteenth century ones referred to at the beginning of this chapter. The examples bear out a common thesis of sociologists about the disrupting effect of industrialization upon the family. That said, we must at once point out that these families are exceptions. Most Woodford men are emphatically not absentee husbands. They hurry back from their offices and factories, arriving between 6 and 7, to spend the evening at home, and they are there for two full days at week-ends. It is their work, especially if rather tedious, which takes second place in their thoughts. They are as devoted as their wives to the house they share. 'In the old days', as one wife said, 'the husband was the husband and the wife was the wife and they each had their own way of going on. Her job was to look after him. The wife wouldn't stand for it nowadays. Husbands help with the children now. They stay more in the home and have more interest in the home.' We shall give some examples of what husbands do in consequence, firstly, in sharing work with their wives, and secondly, in their largely independent domain of house repairing.

Some husbands, as well as doing much of the heavy work in the home, carrying the coals and emptying the rubbish, act as assistants to their wives for at least part of their day. Mr. Hammond 'washes up the dishes every night and lays the

---

[1] The strenuous life of personal competition, long hours, large meals and lack of exercise have been suggested as one reason for the higher mortality of men than women in certain age-groups and classes of the population both in Britain and the United States. The consequence of the high mortality of businessmen in the U.S.A. is that women own most of the nation's wealth, and the same is presumably true in Britain. 'In this patriarchal American culture males preserve their masculinity complex. Striving to live up to the expectation of maleness, men blow out their coronary and cerebral arteries, making wealthy widows out of their wives. Men die five years before women in this country, and women possess 83% of the wealth.' Moloney, J. C., *Symposium on the Healthy Personality*, p. 51. Quoted Titmuss, R. M., 'The Position of Women', p. 96.

breakfast for the morning'. Mr. Clark said that 'on Sunday mornings I usually hoover around for her while she does a bit of washing'. Mr. Davis polishes the floors and helps to make the beds at the week-ends, and during the week takes the dog out for one of his twice-daily walks. So it goes on. In 82% of the 92 married couples in the Woodford old age sample (as compared with 47% of the 98 in Bethnal Green) husbands regularly helped their wives with the housework. We also found, somewhat to our surprise, that gardening was often a joint occupation. If they grew vegetables, this was usually the husband's task, but otherwise they worked literally side by side. This can be illustrated by two brief extracts from diaries. 'Frank dug up a small patch for me to plant a new japonica bush I bought yesterday', one wife reported of her Sunday afternoon, 'I joined him and we planted the bush, hoping it would survive.' 'Spent the afternoon in the garden with John', wrote another, 'We put in the spring bulbs—daffodils, narcissi and tulips. Then I disbudded the chrysan-themums.'

Naturally enough, the couple also share the work, worry and pleasure of the children. 'We have the same routine every night,' said Mrs. Foster. 'I put one child to bed and my husband puts the other. We take it in turns to tell them stories too.' As the children get older and have to take the 11-plus exam, the two parents worry as much as, often more than, their children.

> 'I must admit', Mr. Adams told us, 'my wife and I were having kittens over it. I said to her, "With this confounded 11-plus he'll get his skin trouble again." So we got the doctor to give him a bromide on the day. When he came home from the exam he said, "Dad, this is the most important day in my life." I said, "Son, you couldn't be more wrong—some day you'll get married".'

This sharing of work and interests does not mean that hus-bands are nothing but second mothers, carting the babies about, worrying over the children, doing the shopping and darning the socks. They usually have their own specific tasks within the family economy, particularly in decorating and repairing the home.

The new craftsmanship

We have in our researches seen three stages in this development. In the Bethnal Green of 1956 most people still lived in houses owned by others; men were only just beginning to paper their walls and whitewash the lavatories in their backyards. Yet they were reluctant to undertake any repairs or improvements: they regarded these as the responsibility of the landlord much more readily than he did himself. In Greenleigh, the estate of brand-new houses to which Bethnal Greeners were moved, we saw the access of the 'house-centred' spirit, as we called it. 'The "home" and the family of marriage', we said, 'become the focus of a man's life, as of his wife's, far more completely than in the East End. . . . Their lives outside the family are no longer centred on people; their lives are centred on the house. This change from a people-centred to a house-centred existence is one of the fundamental changes resulting from the migration.'[1]

The third stage is Woodford, or rather the 64% of Woodford people who live in privately-owned houses. Some people in the suburb are, of course, the same in outlook as Bethnal-Greeners, renting houses or flats from private landlords and accepting little responsibility for their condition. A few are in Council houses, as much restricted in what they can do as the tenants of Greenleigh. 'Everything you want to do—you have to submit plans before the Council before you can even build a side-gate. On the rent-book there's a great long list of what you can and can't do. I wanted to keep chickens. There was a regulation size for the hut. The man came down from the Council and he said, no it was going to be four inches too high, four inches! So I had to take out the bricks at the bottom of it.'

Upon the majority, in houses they own themselves, there

---

[1] *Family and Kinship in East London*, p. 119 and p. 127.

are no such restrictions. The lives of the men are even more affected by this than their wives. It was difficult to find any times when they could manage to see us, they were so busy. Here, for example, is what three members of our sample were doing when we finally pinned them down on Saturdays and Sundays in the autumn of 1959.

> Mr. Day, when called upon, said he had been putting together two sheds at the bottom of his garden so that he could have a larger workshop for his bench. It would be useful when he came to put in the central heating system he was planning for the coming winter.

> Mr. Adams, with obvious pride, explained that he had been knocking down the fireplace and chimney breast in a bedroom which was not needed now that he had installed electric storage heaters throughout. He had recently filled in a pond in his garden so that he could have more room for vegetables.

> Mr. Jackson, in his overalls, remarked: 'We're all do-it-yourself people in our family. Since we moved in we've stripped down all the paintwork and redone it in a lighter brown. Now I'm changing the hot-water system around. I've moved the cistern so that it doesn't stick out any more.'

For these three, and most other owner-occupiers, their houses provide almost endless opportunities for work. Cleaning windows, washing down walls, interior painting, repairing house and furniture form an annual routine to set against a five-year plan of improvement and conversion. Each step is discussed in detail with the wife. She does not normally have to do anything. Her role is rather to admire her husband's skill and, occasionally, if a son is not at home, to stand at the bottom of a ladder handing up his power-tool, a pail of size or a box of Rawlplugs.

Why this preoccupation with the house? The first and most obvious reason is sheer pride of ownership. A man who buys his own house has a tiny but independent estate of which he is the undisputed manager. 'I like to be the boss of my own walk,' as one of them said. He can identify himself with his house and feel that as he improves it he is also in a sense adding to his own stature, in the eyes of his wife and his children, his neighbours and himself.

> 'They're all owner-occupiers around here. They've all bought their houses on a mortgage and they take a pride in running a property and keeping up the appearance of their house and garden.'

A second reason is that the house, particularly if old rather than new, is an opportunity for using and developing the capacities of a craftsman. Nobody could be skilled in all the jobs which fall to a modern husband—gardener, painter, paper-hanger, plasterer, carpenter, plumber, concreter, electrician, motor mechanic. But quite often he can pick up a good layman's knowledge of at least some of these trades, mainly through trial and error, partly by reading do-it-yourself and gardening magazines, partly under instruction from relatives and other men at work. The work of the day, in office or factory, may be becoming more and more boring not for the executives we mentioned earlier who hire builders instead of being them, but, as their work gets more specialized, for their employees. To compensate for this, the work of the night or week-end may be becoming psychologically more and more rewarding as it gets more generalized, more skilled and more creative. The higher incomes and shorter hours generated by increasing division of labour provide new outlets in the home for 'conspicuous production'. These husbands can afford the paint-rollers, metal ladders and tool chests on sale in the handyman's shops of Woodford.

The third reason is that the house is regarded as a sort of business. Economic calculation goes like this. Buying your own house actually saves money in the long run. 'To rent is a waste of money—you get nothing back.' 'If you're buying a house you're saving at the same time. You're not paying out rent and nothing to show for it—you've got something to show for it at the end.' Interest and amortization on a mortgage may be a good deal higher than rent for similar accommodation—if you could get it. But you do have the satisfaction of knowing that the difference is helping to give you an asset for your old age or (where the mortgage is supported by an insurance policy) for your wife and children should you not last as long as the mortgage.

You then work out how much money you are saving by doing your own work instead of getting builders to do it for you. 'I got an estimate for a decorating job recently, just to see what it would cost, and they wanted £34. Folks don't get that much money these days, not middle-class folk anyway. Only working-class people do.' Mr. Prior demonstrated at once his business acumen and his sense of class superiority. And finally you estimate how much you have augmented the value of the property by your expenditure of labour, skill and money. Mr Bates was so sure of himself that when he changed jobs recently he took eight months' holiday, lived on his savings and made an 'investment' in his house. He knocked walls down to make larger rooms, he rebuilt and re-equipped the kitchen with a steel sink unit, built-in cupboards and Marley tiles, he erected a garage and a conservatory screened by pink venetian blinds. Looking on it purely as a commercial proposition, let alone anything else, he was very well satisfied with results. 'I made these vast improvements and now I hope to make at least £1,000 on the property if it's sold.' Owners notice the selling prices of nearby houses—knowledge of these often circulates freely up and down the road. They notice that in the long-sustained inflation of the last twenty years prices have been rising steadily. They know that, provided they maintain it in good condition, the value of their asset is increasing. Add on a bit extra for improvements, and they can at the end feel very content with their one-man business.

We began this chapter by recalling that the agricultural or handicraft family of the past was also a partnership in husbandry between man and wife. Has industrialization destroyed this kind of family? A common view is that as one by one functions have been transferred from the home, the domestic partnership has been weakened. All we can say is that such a view is certainly not confirmed by what we have seen and heard in this London suburb. If we are right, the process of removing functions from the domestic to the general economy has been halted. It is surely plain enough that technology has in its later phases reintroduced jobs into the home—ice-cream manufacture has come back with the refrigerator, laundering with the washing machine and entertainment with television. These affect women and children even more than men. But what struck us most was the way in which the wealth which advancing technology yields is being increasingly used to support the new cult of the amateur handyman. He is as busy keeping up with rapidly changing fashions of interior decoration and design as his wife is kept absorbed in conforming to rising and ever-changing standards of child-care, cookery and dress. More money is used for the house, more leisure used for work. The husbandman of England is back in a new form, as horticulturist rather than agriculturist, as builder rather than cattleman, as improver not of a strip of arable land but of the semi-detached family estate at 33 Ellesmere Road.

III

GENERATIONS APART

In the East End, despite a growing partnership between husbands and wives, the relatives were not excluded; the wider family still flourished; the wife had a mother by her as well as her husband. After marriage couples did not move to a new area, but went on living 'up the street' or 'round the corner' from their parents. Things would obviously be different in a suburb like Woodford. But how different? In this chapter we try to answer that question from the standpoint of young married couples.

We asked everybody in the general sample whether their parents were living, and, if so, where. The answers given by married people are compared for the two districts in Table I. Here, as elsewhere, unless otherwise stated, 'married' includes widowed and divorced. As expected, far more Bethnal Greeners live close to their parents. As for Woodford, most people's parents live right outside the borough, even though, with about 12,000 more people and over five times the area, it is much larger than Bethnal Green. Of those parents living outside Woodford, just over a third live within five miles, in places like Leyton, Walthamstow, East Ham and Ilford, and just under a third more than 100 miles away.

Most of these couples are relative newcomers—of the 394 married people in the general sample with parents alive, nearly half have been in Woodford less than ten years, and another quarter between ten and twenty. They moved *into* Woodford, and away from their parents.

Why? One reason is straightforward enough—the job. Mr. Franklin, for instance, is a quantity surveyor, who lived

TABLE I

PROXIMITY OF PARENTS—WOODFORD AND BETHNAL GREEN

(General samples—married people with at least one parent alive)

Parents' Residence	*Woodford*	*Bethnal Green*
Same dwelling	9%	12%
Within five minutes' walk ..	7%	29%
Elsewhere in the same borough	15%	13%
Outside the same borough	69%	46%
Total %	100%	100%
Number	394	369

The results of tests of significance of this and subsequent tables are given in Appendix 5.

in a small Yorkshire town near his wife's family for a year after their marriage. He wanted to stay there to suit his wife. But as he was unable to get a job with decent prospects he came to London, and chose Woodford to live because he had relatives there. Mr. Humphreys is a local government official who moved in from Bedford after he had been successful in getting a more senior post in the Town Hall of a neighbouring Essex borough. Yet another is Mr. King, a business manager living in Wanstead, who had been in charge of a factory at Brentwood until he was promoted to his firm's main works at Stratford. 'I had to move then,' he explained, 'I have to be near to my factories.'

These three, like most of those whose work had brought them to Woodford, had managerial or professional occupations. This is, after all, not surprising—in the country generally, their jobs force movement upon the middle classes. The manager has to move from factory to factory; the professional man to go here for training and there for work; the executive to travel as his company dictates. This greater mobility of people in white-collar occupations is evident in Woodford, where 35% of the 580 middle-class people in the general sample, against 25% of the 355 working-class, were residents of less than ten years' standing. Other research has shown differences even more marked in the country as a whole. According to one survey, during a period of four years, 31% of 'professional and salaried' people and 22% of 'black-coated' had moved into a different district, against 12% of skilled manual workers, and 8% of semi-skilled and unskilled.[1] Such movement may be less necessary for the native of Greater London, who has a vast range of occupational opportunities at the other end of the Underground, than for the person whose home is in Banbury or Wolverhampton or Nelson.

Job was not the only reason though. For Mr. Davis, a Civil Servant, work followed home rather than the other way round. 'My first post was at Cambridge', he said, 'We lived in furnished rooms there for two years. Then, through a friend, we got the offer of an unfurnished flat in Woodford and I applied for a transfer to London.'

The Londoners often kept the same jobs; but they wanted the space and air of Woodford. 'We were living in our own house in Poplar', said Mr. Phillips, 'and we thought we'd like to move into a better area for the children.' 'I think', said Mrs. Archer, who is also buying her house, 'that Woodford's much nicer than further in where I used to live with my parents. It's more spacious and much nicer altogether.'

Many people had not specially chosen Woodford as a district, but a house which happened to be there.

'Before we settled on this house', said Mr. Burgess, 'we looked at more than 200 houses in Ilford, Loughton, all over the

---

[1] Douglas, J. W. B., and Blomfield, J. M., *Children Under Five*, p. 27. See also *Social Implications of the 1947 Mental Survey*, and Newton, M. P., and Jeffery, J. R., *Internal Migration*.

place. It wasn't easy to find just what we wanted. We wanted something detached but not too detached. A big enough house, but at a moderate price. We eventually chose this one.'

'When we bought this place,' Mrs. Ashwood explained, 'it wasn't very easy to get houses, and we had to look around quite a lot to find one at a price we could afford in something like the sort of district we wanted on this side of London.'

'We looked at different houses and chose this one', said Mr. White, 'we didn't specially want to come to Woodford; it just seemed to me a good property.'

Suburban attitudes

In Woodford most couples did not expect to live near the older generation. Other things were uppermost in their minds. For instance, most people—certainly most of the middle-class ones who were from outside London—took it for granted that the husband's job was the first consideration of all. Mr. Burgess, a company secretary, said, 'A man's got to go where his work is, and a wife's got to go where her husband's livelihood is. You just can't stay near your parents if your job pulls in another direction.' Some of the parents themselves made the same point. 'I wish they lived nearer', Mrs. Arrell said of her daughters, 'but you must go where your living is, mustn't you?' 'My daughter in Liverpool', said Mrs. Thomas, 'has to be there because of her husband's business.' 'He had to be prepared to move about for promotion,' said Mrs. Crombie of her son living in Birmingham, 'It wasn't my affair'. Mrs. Best, the wife of a retired head teacher, said about her daughter in Southern Rhodesia:

> 'We miss seeing her and the baby, but children must make their own lives. We would hate it if they stayed hanging around our apron-strings. If his situation takes them to Southern Rhodesia, well and good. They must go. They mustn't be tied to their parents.'

Whether they came from London or not, whichever generation they belonged to, this was a common refrain—that the children had their own lives to lead, that their independence should be welcomed and indeed encouraged, and that it was wrong for parents to try to hang on to their children after marriage. 'My family's got a motto', said Mr. Archer, 'When you're married you're on your own.' And Mrs. Liversidge, two of whose children had moved away from the district, said, 'I'd be broken-hearted if I thought I'd done anything to prevent them going off and becoming people in their own right. I think that this possessiveness and tying them to you all the time is wrong.' 'You shouldn't delve into your children's lives', Mrs. Easton remarked.

There were others, again in both generations, who went further and argued that it was positively a mistake for parents and children to live too near. 'A couple ought to move right away from their parents', said Mr. Humphreys, 'If they live in the same area, the parents can exercise an enormous influence. That's wrong.' 'I think it's better to be away from them', Mrs. King said, 'Not too far, but far enough so that your mother can't pop in every day.' What a contrast with the East End! There it is expected and welcomed that mother and daughter *will* 'pop in every day', and sometimes all day as well.

No one suggested that children should cut themselves off from their parents entirely; many had in mind, as the best sort of distance, one which allowed regular contact without threatening independence. 'When you get married', as Mr. Matthews put it, 'you ought to move away a sufficient distance not to be on their doorstep, but within visiting distance because they like to see the children growing up.' Opinions differed about how far this ideal distance was. Mrs. Martin, whose parents had recently moved from Carlisle to Cromer, still over 100 miles from Woodford, said, 'I wouldn't like to live too near to them. Where they are now is just about right. Carlisle was a bit too far, because we couldn't go to see them very often, but now we can go to see them more and they can come to see us.' Mrs. Morris, whose son lives at Morden in South London, said, 'That little bit of distance keeps the situation in true balance. If they were near enough to pop round the corner they might lean on me too much.'

And Mr. Stockman, with a son four miles away at Newbury Park, said, 'That's just a nice distance. We can live our own lives but still keep in touch.' If opinions differed about the distance, there was something like agreement on the one proposition that couples should not live close by parents after their wedding.

Seeing relatives

'Keeping in touch'—it was something people wanted to do if at all possible. But what does this mean in practice? So far, we have found that far fewer couples than in the East End live close to parents, and have said nothing of how much they actually see of them. Table II, again comparing Woodford and Bethnal Green, shows how much husbands and wives taken together see of their mothers.(See Table XXXIX in Appendix 4 for contacts with fathers.)

TABLE II

CONTACTS WITH MOTHERS—WOODFORD AND BETHNAL GREEN

(General samples—married people with mothers alive)

	Woodford	*Bethnal Green*
Seen within previous 24 hours	30%	43%
Seen earlier in previous week	33%	31%
Not seen within previous week	37%	26%
Total with mothers alive % ..	100%	100%
Number	346	290

There is a clear variation between the two places, but less marked than the difference in where parents live. Nearly two-thirds of the married people with mothers alive had, after all, seen them at some time in the previous week, and in fact only about a fifth (19%) had seen them *less* than a month previously. Certainly, despite distance, most young couples make a point of maintaining fairly regular contact with their parents.

At the same time couples in Woodford *do* see their parents a good deal less than those in Bethnal Green. It is the same with brothers and sisters, who also live farther away and are seen less frequently. Of the 2,110 siblings of married people in the Woodford general sample, 23% were seen in the previous week, against 35% of the 2,722 siblings of married Bethnal Greeners.[1] We are also sure enough in our own minds that this evidence on contacts understates the differences between the two places. For one thing, when mother and daughter, or two sisters, do see each other every day, it is usually just once, not the popping in and out, the constant mingling of daily living, so common in the East End. For another, a few Woodford people have one or even two relatives as neighbours, but they hardly ever have a dozen, a score or more, as do many East Enders. In Bethnal Green married couples often belong to what we called on a previous occasion the 'extended family', that is to a 'combination of families who to some large degree form one domestic unit'.[2] Mrs. Cole, one of our Bethnal Green informants, belonged to one of these and her account of her day showed just how close relationships can be in the East End.[3]

> 'After breakfast I bath the baby and sweep the kitchen, and wash up. Then I go up the road shopping with Mum, Greta (one of the wife's married sisters who also has a child) and the three children. After dinner I clean up and then round about two o'clock I go out for a walk if it's fine with Mum and Greta and the children. I come back at about a quarter to four to be in time for Janice when she gets back from school. She calls in at Mum's on her way just to see if I'm there. This is an ordinary day. If anything goes wrong and I'm in any trouble I always go running round to Mum's.'

[1] Fuller data on residence of siblings and contacts with them are given in Tables XL and XLI, Appendix 4.
[2] *Family and Kinship in East London,* p. 32.
[3] Ibid, p. 30.

These localized 'extended families'—family groups spreading over two or more nearby houses—are the distinctive feature of kinship in the East End. In Woodford they are rare.

This is one important contrast between the districts. Far less people in Woodford live very close to parents and other relatives, and there is less day-to-day interaction. Meetings between relatives are much less casual, much more dependent upon definite appointments. 'We don't see our parents except by arrangement', explained Mr. Humphreys, 'It's better that way.' Mrs. Ashwood herself summed it up as we do ourselves: 'I think relatives are more important in East Enders' lives than they are to people like us.'

This chapter, written from the standpoint of young husbands and wives, shows that the wider family does not flourish in the suburb as it does in the East End. The immediate family—the married couple with their dependent children—is much more on its own, more independent, more self-sufficient. These differences are obviously due in part to the class composition of the two districts. But we will not at this stage explore the influence of social class in any detail. This is left over until Chapter VII, where we look into the differences between the social classes within Woodford. Meanwhile, all that we have established is that, for young couples generally, kinship plays a far smaller part than in Bethnal Green.

IV

ARE THE PARENTS DESERTED?

THE looseness of kinship ties described in the last chapter may not matter much to the younger generation, may even be a positive advantage for them. The implications for the old are more serious. The principal finding of Townsend's study of old age was that old people in Bethnal Green were supported and cared for by their children. One of the main functions of the East End extended family was to care for its older members, and its importance far over-shadowed the formal social services. This, it seems on the evidence so far, can hardly be true of the suburb. If children live apart from their parents, then the parents presumably have to get along without their help. Old people, we thought, might prove to be more often isolated, more often excluded from the family circle, and, if they were, their plight might prove a distinctive feature of the suburban, middle-class way of life. We should explain that, in presenting material on this subject from both the general survey and the old age sample, we have followed the earlier Bethnal Green study of old age and counted as 'old' people who have passed the official 'pensionable age' (60 for women, 65 for men). We shall begin with old people who have children.

Before we look at old people's relationships with their married offspring, and ask where these live, we should say just a word about their single children. Are they living with their parents? Of the 210 people in the old age sample, 47 had at least one unmarried child, and they had 58 unmarried children altogether between them (that is, children who had *never* married—widowed and divorced children are included

36

with the 'married'). The majority of these bachelors and spinsters turned out to be still at home with their parents—of the 58, only three daughters and eight sons were away from home, and three of the sons were away only temporarily—two in the Forces, and one at university. The proportion of single people living at home was almost exactly the same as in Bethnal Green. In so far as they benefited from having children at home, old people in the suburb were as well off as those in the East End.

Now for the married children. The previous chapter showed that married couples live away from their parents. Does this mean that old people live at a distance from their married children? Table III shows how near their nearest married child was, comparing Woodford with Bethnal Green.

TABLE III

PROXIMITY OF NEAREST MARRIED CHILD TO PEOPLE OF PENSION AGE IN WOODFORD AND BETHNAL GREEN

(General samples—people of pensionable age with at least one married child)

	Woodford	*Bethnal Green*
Same dwelling	23%	21%
Within five minutes' walk ..	17%	32%
Elsewhere in same borough	22%	8%
Outside borough	38%	39%
Total %	100%	100%
Number	109	131

The surprise of this table, and perhaps the greatest surprise of the whole report, is that the two places are so alike. More people in Bethnal Green have a married child living within five minutes' walk, more in Woodford have one elsewhere in the same borough. Otherwise, the differences between the places are not at all sharp. If we consider how often people *see* their children, rather than where they live, even these differences virtually disappear. The proportions of old people with married children seeing at least one of them in the previous day was 56% in Woodford, 58% in Bethnal Green. In both places a further 25% had seen a married child at some other time in the previous week. In suburb and city alike, over four-fifths of the old people with married children had seen one or more at least once in the previous week. The old people of the suburb are plainly as much in touch with children, measured in this way, as those in the East End.

The life cycle of kinship

This conclusion is not at all what might have been predicted from the last chapter. Indeed, the two sets of findings, first from the viewpoint of the young and then from that of the old, appear, on the face of it, to contradict each other. Do they?

Part of the explanation is that while all the young people of the last chapter could have only one father and mother, many of the parents considered in this chapter had more than one child. What we have shown in this chapter is that many Woodford parents, while they may be far away from most of their children, do live close to one of them.[1] The other part of the explanation is that 'parents' has meant different things in the two chapters. In the previous chapter we were concerned with all parents, here only with those parents who are *over* pension age. But the parents of many husbands and wives are younger; of the 346 people in the general sample with mothers living, nearly a third (30%) had mothers below the age of 60, and of the 234 with fathers living, nearly half (47%) had fathers below 65. If the relationship is different between the younger parents and their married children, this could

[1] Woodford old people had far less children than those in the East End. Of the 149 married or widowed people of pension age in the Woodford general sample, only 16% had four or more children, against 47% of the 149 Bethnal Green old people. But the important thing is that *one* child was near as often in the one district as the other.

account, at least in part, for the apparent contradiction. Table IV makes it clear that age is crucial. The table again shows the proximity of the nearest married child both in Woodford and Bethnal Green, but this time compares people in the general sample *below* pensionable age with those above it.

TABLE IV

PROXIMITY OF NEAREST MARRIED CHILD TO PEOPLE BELOW AND ABOVE PENSION AGE, IN WOODFORD AND BETHNAL GREEN

(General samples—people with at least one married child)

	Woodford		Bethnal Green	
	People below Pension Age	People above Pension Age	People below Pension Age	People above Pension Age
Same dwelling ..	10%	23%	24%	21%
Within five minutes	6%	17%	23%	32%
Elsewhere in same borough ..	21%	22%	10%	8%
Outside borough	63%	38%	43%	39%
Total % ..	100%	100%	100%	100%
Number ..	119	109	146	131

The figures show one key difference between the two districts. In Bethnal Green the proportion of people with a married child living in the same house or within five minutes' walk is much the same after as before pension age: in Woodford it more than doubles. And, once more, the differences are reflected in the frequency with which children are seen. In Bethnal Green, 57% of the people below, and 58% of those above, pension age had seen a married child in the previous

39

day. In Woodford, the proportion was 36% of those below, 56% of those above, pension age.

We have only divided people at the pension age because this is how it has been done in other studies. The same general conclusion emerges if we disregard this rather arbitrary division, and compare people in their fifties with people in their sixties, seventies and eighties. This is done in Table V. It shows that the older the parents the more often they live in the same dwelling as a married child. There is a similar tendency for older parents (at any rate up to the age of 70) to live *near* their children if they do not actually live *with* them.

TABLE V

PEOPLE OF DIFFERENT AGES IN WOODFORD LIVING WITH MARRIED CHILDREN

(General sample—people with at least one married child)

	Age of Parents			
	59 and under	*60–69*	*70–79*	*80 and over*
Percentage living in same dwelling as married child ..	12%	11%	25%	41%
Total number ..	101	55	49	17

This variation with age is largely, though not wholly, explained by widowhood. Of the 40 widowed men and women in the general sample who were over pension age and had married children, 42% lived with one of them, against 16% of the 69 people whose spouse was still alive.[1]

[1] A special analysis of a 20% sample of the 1951 Census returns for Wanstead and Woodford, carried out for us by the General Register Office, provided confirmation. The Census dealt with *households*, not the whole dwelling, but the figures show the same trend. Of 913 married people of pension age, 10% lived in the same household as a married child, against 33% of the 619 widowed and divorced.

The contrast between the districts is that in one, the generations are together throughout life; in the other, they separate when the children marry but rejoin each other when the parents grow old. The life cycle of kinship follows a different course in the two places. Just how this comes about is something we shall now try to describe.

As many as three-quarters of these married children had joined up with their parents to provide help or company. Sometimes it was illness or infirmity that had made extra care necessary. Mr. Beaver, for instance, was now an invalid requiring constant nursing. 'Four years ago', said Mrs. Beaver, 'I asked Jean if she'd like to come to live here, mainly because of my husband's illness. I couldn't have managed on my own.' Mr. and Mrs. Crombie are another couple, both over 80. 'When my eyes failed me', Mrs. Crombie explained, 'we couldn't really manage on our own any longer, and my daughter and her husband took this house so that we could have a couple of rooms in it.'

But death is the common catalyst. Sometimes the house is too big and too lonely for the parent widowed, and then either the child comes to the parent, as happened to Mrs. Fane, or the parent moves in with the child, as Mrs. Clements did. 'My husband died in 1956', said Mrs. Fane, 'and my son and his family came to live with me soon after. It didn't seem right to have this whole house on my own. We have all lived together ever since.' 'During the war I was living alone in the old house in Romford', said Mrs. Clements, 'A bomb dropped in a field near to where I was living. It scared me and my daughter said I was silly to live alone, so I came here. It was more for company really.' More commonly the old widow or widower needs looking after. Mr. Collis and Mrs. Lucas are two examples. 'My wife died five years ago,' said Mr. Collis, 'I carried on here for a while with my youngest son and my daughter Vera used to come in every week to do anything that needed doing. Then, when my son got married, Vera asked if she could come and live here and look after me. I agreed straight away, you can be sure.' 'The real reason we live together', Mrs. Lucas' daughter said, 'is Mum's health. After Dad died she had trouble with her heart, and as well as that she'd had a cataract—and she's a bit deaf. Her doctor said she shouldn't really live alone. It's better for her like this.'

A quarter of the married children at home had never left their parents at all. They had stayed on because there was room for them, while waiting for a house of their own. 'When Edna got married', said Mrs. Crisp, 'they couldn't seem to find a place and when she asked if they could stay on here I said yes.' As in Bethnal Green, in large families much depended on whether the child was the last to marry. Usually they could be accommodated only if they were.

> 'When we first came here', said Mrs. Clarkson, 'my eldest son was the only one married and the rest of us all lived here together like we had in the old house back in Shoreditch. Then Fred married and moved away to Chingford—and then Edith—she went to Barkingside. So when Dorothy got married just after the war, I said she could stay on here.'

Dorothy is still there. With her mother needing constant care, she felt she could not leave now even if she wanted to. Mrs. Anstead's daughter was another similarly placed: 'We never intended to stay here', she explained, 'we always said we'd get a place of our own, but it never worked out like that. And now, of course, with mother like she is, we couldn't possibly go.'

Whatever the details of the story, the plot was essentially the same. The parent or parents needed care or companionship, and one at least of their children had supplied it. The family's readiness to care for old age is apparently not confined to places like the East End.

Problem of sharing

What we have said does not for a moment imply that relations between aged parents and their children are the same in the two places. One big difference we have already noted—most Bethnal Green parents have been near their children all along; in Woodford they have not. This is important in many ways—for one thing, the reason why so many old people live with children in Woodford is, paradoxically, because they used to live so far away. The old people of Bethnal Green were down the street; their children had only to walk over the road to look after them or keep them company. But Woodford children lived so far off that even with cars they could not keep an eye on parents all the time, nor give them that assurance which old people need, of someone close by to call on in an emergency. As Mrs. Green said, 'My mother was living up in Liverpool when my father died last year, and we invited her to come and live with us. She was such a long way away up there. You wouldn't mind her living on her own if she was near.'

Where can they come to, except right into their children's homes? Most Woodford people own their homes and do not want to sell them to move away to their parents, even if their jobs allowed. The parents had to leave their homes instead. Of the 52 people in the old age sample living with married children, nearly half (23) had gone to live in the child's home, against only three of the 39 in Bethnal Green. Another seven in Woodford had moved with their children into a new and larger house bought especially for its suitability for sharing.

This arrangement may be much better for the parents than living on their own. But it raises problems all the same, of a sort which are much more rare in the East End. The parents have come from Sheffield, Rochester, Edmonton, Epping, and have to put up with a strange new district, at an age when they are not at their most adaptable. Even if they have moved to their children from as near as Walthamstow, like Mrs. Connelly, they do not know their new neighbours: 'I don't go out much', she said, 'because I don't really know anybody round here. All my real friends are over at Walthamstow.'

Sharing may also raise acute problems for the younger generation. Mrs. Eton said flatly, 'It doesn't matter how good you are or how helpful you are, there's bound to be trouble if you're sharing with parents.' 'Occasionally I long to escape', said one daughter, 'It gets a bit of a strain. I can never go out.' The children's resentment is understandable if they have to act nurse as well as companion to old people who cannot go upstairs except on all fours, who are always up in the middle of the night clattering about in the kitchen making cups of tea, or who imagine that their children are plotting to starve them. These were three examples given to us. Another illustration is provided by Mrs. Anstead who lives with her only daughter.

> 'Her health is all right generally', said the daughter, 'but she can't get about as well as she used to as her mind wanders sometimes—she finds it hard to concentrate. She is a problem. You feel you owe an obligation to your mother, but on the other hand you feel you would like a little relief sometimes. You're pulled both ways—you've got obligations to your mother, of course, but you've got obligations to your husband and your own family too. Sometimes it does create tension.'

A crucial question is, who is in command? However hard the children try to compromise, they are bound to expect their parents to adjust to the ways of the household, to accept its customs, rather than the other way round. No wonder a parent complains. From being head of her own home, she (or he) is now lodger in someone else's. 'It's not like having your own front door', said Mrs. Lacey, 'When you've been used to having your own home, it's very difficult to settle down and watch things going on and not interfere.' 'They don't want you to interfere', said another, 'and it's the hardest thing sometimes to stand by and see something done you know is wrong.' 'I can't have people in,' complained Mrs. Casbolt, 'because it's not my home, it's my daughter's.' From the point of view of the younger generation, one son complained about his mother, who had come to live with them:

> 'She doesn't seem to feel she's sharing in with us. She seems to want to keep her independence. She won't join in and accept our ways. I feel she should try to *integrate* herself more with the family.'

44

In such a setting old people may feel more on their own than if they were a hundred miles away.[1] 'You feel in the way sometimes', said Mrs. Welch, 'You feel you're not wanted.'

The tension is almost inevitable. The parent is whirled off into someone else's house. The someone else is not strange, but the house is, the daily round is, the relationship is, of being subordinate rather than mistress. In Bethnal Green, the old do not have to endure such a shock. The elderly mothers have some of the qualities of a matriarch, and these they retain far into their old age, respected by their children for their wisdom and for the struggles they once waged against hardship and poverty. The relationship is a continuing one, and a daily one, without any sudden breaks—away into independence, back into dependence. And when they live anyway in the same street they do not need to put up with all the strains of living with their children merely in order to be assured of some modicum of care. As far as the old go, there is little doubt they are in a less enviable position in Woodford.

Some of the strain of 'living on top of each other' can be eased, of course, if the parents have their own separate accommodation within the house, particularly when the older generation is represented by a married couple instead of a widowed person. The old and the young can then each lead a partially independent life. 'It works out very well', said Mr. Bartrop, 'but it only works if you've got your own bit of space and your own place to go to. That way you can go there when you feel you can't stand being with the others and you're very friendly and happy when you do see each other.' 'They've got their half of the house and we've got ours', explained Mrs. Bakewell, 'That way there's no argy-bargy and no nasty feelings. We can live our own lives and not feel we're being a bother to each other: we can be independent *and* friendly.' Mrs. Benson said, 'My daughter and her

---

[1] A U.S. report remarks on a similar problem in that country. 'One of the commonest social complaints of older persons living within the households of children is the feeling of isolation within the family group.' *Five Hundred Over Sixty*. Kutner, B., *et. al.*, p. 110.

husband have got their own sitting-room. It's better like that, isn't it?' In fact, just under half of the people in the old age sample sharing with married children lived in the same household—in the sense of eating and fully sharing with them—and these were, in the main, the widowed or infirm. The others preserved an independent household within the shared dwelling.

Parents as neighbours

In view of the difficulties of living together, it is not surprising that many people would prefer to share a neighbourhood with their parents—to have them living near, rather than in the same house. As Sheldon said in his classic study of old age in Wolverhampton, that is the pattern preferred if it is at all possible.[1] But, of course, in Woodford it is not easy. In Bethnal Green, proximity is ensured by the mother whose influence with the landlord secures a place nearby for her daughter. In Woodford, it means finding and buying another house nearby in the same locality, and the right house at the right price cannot always be found. Just the same, many people did succeed in achieving this. As we showed at the beginning of the chapter, the proportion of old people who had a married child living within five minutes' walk rose from 6% before pension age to 17% after it.

Usually it depended on the efforts of the children. Mr. Carter was an example. He was determined not to live with his mother-in-law if he could avoid it, and yet had to accommodate to his wife's insistence upon being in the same street as her mother, who had been seriously ill. He would have liked to move to a job in Scotland, but could not because he would have had to take his mother-in-law with him. He instructed all the estate agents in Wanstead to let him know of any large houses being put up for sale in Pinner Road, where the mother lived, money being of little concern, as he was a wealthy business manager. Within six months he was informed of such a house, and moved in to the congratulations of his wife

[1] Sheldon, J. H., *The Social Medicine of Old Age*, pp. 195–6.

and the relief of her mother. The Jacksons were equally fortunate. Mrs. Jackson's parents had not yet become infirm, but she wanted to be well placed to help them when they did. So when the woman in the house next door told her one morning over the fence that she and her husband were going to Southend, Mrs. Jackson immediately persuaded her husband to put in a bid for it. He succeeded in buying the house privately without the intervention of an estate agent, saving the expense of the commission, and his in-laws from Hackney are now installed next door.

Another example was Mrs. Rogers. After Mr. Rogers died, she decided to sell the large Sussex house in which her family had been raised, and move in with her son, David, in Woodford. Mrs. Rogers used part of the money from the sale to build another bedroom on to the back of David's house and an extension to his kitchen. They did not get on together as well as she had hoped. When the next-door house fell vacant and was put up for sale, David suggested that his mother should buy it, and this she did, paying with the money she still had left over from the Sussex sale. Mrs. Rogers is now living there with an unmarried daughter.

It is not always the children who take the initiative. Mr. Easton, for instance, is a builder and when each of his four children married he gave them a house as a sort of dowry. The children specified the kind of houses they wanted; he built and paid for them, and, in doing so, ensured that none of them would be far away. For one of his daughters he bought a plot of land next to his own, so she lives, although in her own house, almost on his little estate.[1] Mr. and Mrs. Williams scoured the district near them for a house of the right kind and at the right price for their son-in-law. 'We didn't exactly find it for our daughter, but well, they were looking for a house to buy, and had their names down at estate agents all over Woodford. We actually found it for them while they were away on holiday. The estate agent was

---

[1] Sheldon observed that in Wolverhampton, 4% of his sample of old people actually lived next door to one of their children. Sheldon, J. H., op. cit., p. 195.

a friend of theirs and he told us it was going; we asked him to hold on to it till they got back from holiday and they took it.'

Where parents and children are living near to each other they may form an 'extended family' very like those we previously described in Bethnal Green. Mrs. Topham used to be in domestic service. Now she lives alone in a tiny gas-lit cottage. The room is dominated by a very large Victorian print of a maiden on her way to bed, her golden hair loose about her shoulders, a candle throwing a warm glow over her face and one naked shoulder. 'My family', she said, 'have had the tenancy of this house for seventy years. You see, we've been Wanstead people for ages back. My mother was christened, married, and buried in the little church near the golf club. Her family and their family before them were here.' Her daughter lives a few streets away and is seen every day, often several times. Her daughter takes all her washing to do at her house and brings her over many meals. The two granddaughters came in during the interview, as they often do after school. Mrs. Topham is very attached to them both because they were born in her house, and she helped to care for them when they were babies.

Mr. Randall, a retired surveyor, also belongs to an extended family. His day, as he described it himself in his diary, is very much mixed up with his daughter's. He visits her home constantly. 'Bicycled up to my daughter Joan. I usually go to lunch with her when my sister is at work. She was in the middle of cooking dinner so I went to the baker's for bread and two tins of food for the cat. Up the Green I ran into my friend Arthur and had a chat. Said cheerio and went back to my daughter. She was still getting dinner ready and as there was nobody to talk to I went into the lounge and strummed on the piano. I suppose I must have been idling at the piano, playing from memory, for well over half an hour when there was a shout from my son-in-law Frank of "Dinner-ho, Pop" and the four of us sat down to chop, new potatoes, peas and brussels sprouts—and very nice it was. My grandson, Alan, was full of beans as usual and it was not long before he said "Want to hear my latest record?" "Yes," I said, "if it is not a long player." It was a record of some of Chopin's pianoforte music and we both enjoyed it. He is a Beethoven fan and he and I get on well together, more so than his sister Janet—as we seem to like classical music of same musicians while Janet is more of the Rock and Roll.'

The interviews with the marriage sample also provided some examples of extended families. Mr. Foster's parents live at Westcliff and he sees them only two or three times a year. But his wife's live in Woodford, 'just round the corner'. 'The wife sees her mother practically every day', Mr. Foster explained, 'She usually comes in the afternoon and stays until about eight, so I see her when I get back from work.' When Mrs. Foster is ill, her mother comes in to help and 'if we go out it's usually her who looks after the children for us.' Asked what he had done on the previous Sunday, Mr. Foster said, 'We went round for dinner and tea to my mother-in-law's', adding with a laugh, 'She seems to pop up a lot, doesn't she?' Mrs. Chambers is another of the younger women with parents living nearby. 'My parents live about three minutes' walk away', she told us, 'And I see them every day.' Recounting what had happened on the day before the interview Mrs. Chambers said, 'After tea I drove my youngest daughter to her piano lesson. On the way back I called in on my mother and father because, having been shopping up to the West End in the afternoon, I hadn't seen them during the day.'

Mrs. Foster and Mrs. Chambers are exceptions among the younger women. But among the older parents it is the minority who do not belong to some kind of continuing family group, whether in the one house or spread over several. This difference between young and old provides the main contrast with the East End, and the principal conclusion of this chapter. On the whole, it is an encouraging one. There are, of course, strains and worries for both young and old; the parents, in particular, often have to sacrifice their independence for companionship and care. But the fact remains

that, in ill-health, infirmity or widowhood, the aged parents
are, by and large, cared for by their children. Asked what use
she made of various social services, Mrs. Broadbent said, 'It's
unnecessary while you've got children, isn't it ?' Kinship may
mean less in the suburb at other stages in life, but in old age,
when the need arises, the family is once more the main source
of support. The old felt they could call on their children, the
children that they *should* respond. 'When they've brought you
up', said Mr. Burgess, 'you feel you've got a certain amount
of moral obligation to them.' This sense of filial duty is as
strong in one district as another.

V

GROWING OLD WITHOUT CHILDREN

ONCE in need of care, the old, it seems, are no more neglected in Woodford than in Bethnal Green. But to this statement there must, on the evidence produced so far, be one big qualification. The people we were describing in the last chapter all had children alive. They were the fortunate ones. We still have to discuss those without children—the single people, the widows and widowers who either never had children or whose children died before them. Is isolation common amongst them? In general, relatives of Woodford people are more scattered and seen less often. This apparently does not matter so much for parents with children to fall back on, but for others it might be crucial.

In order to be sure of what we were talking about we needed larger numbers of single old people than our own samples would supply. We therefore asked the General Register Office for help, and a 20% sample of people of pension age from the 1951 Census returns for Woodford was analysed specially for us. It shows, with more statistical authority than our samples would allow, that only a minority of single old people live alone. Of the 242 single people of pension age, 53% lived in the same household as relatives, 26% with friends, and only 21% by themselves. Since the Census only deals with *households*, and excludes other people who may be living in the same house but eating separately, these figures understate the proportion sharing a house with relatives.

The single people in the old age sample illustrate what 'living with relatives' can mean. Out of the 210 people interviewed in that sample, 25 were single. Most of these—actually all but three—were women; they belonged to the generation whose potential husbands were killed in the 1914–18 war. Many of them shared a home with someone else, usually a sister, or brother. Of the 25, 11 (ten of them spinsters) were living with siblings. One is Miss Beale, aged 69, who actually lives with two siblings—a spinster sister and a bachelor brother. They have been together all their lives, having stayed on in their present home when their parents died. The two sisters do the laundry, shopping, cleaning and cooking, taking it in turns to go on holiday so that there is always someone to look after the brother, who does not like going away. He does the gardening, painting and decorating, everything except the wallpaper which his hand is not steady enough to hang.

Miss Ley lives with a sister. She illustrates not only how single sisters share a home, but also how married siblings provide the single with links to other relatives—mainly nephews and nieces or grand-nephews and grand-nieces—whom they then treat almost as their own children.

Although the house outside is like so many others, with bay windows and a covered porch, indoors it has a quiet Victorian air. One painting shows Highland cattle, another giant cart-horses led by boys in smocks, another a posy of pansies and roses. The photographs on the mantelpiece are of nieces and nephews. Miss Ley lives with Florence, an unmarried sister, who was left the house by a bachelor brother whom she'd looked after all her life. Florence does the cooking and shopping, and Miss Ley cleans her own bedroom and kitchen, and manages to keep the other rooms tidy—'My heart's weak, you see, so I'm not able to do really heavy work.' 'It's not good to be single when you get old,' she said, 'I love children. I brought up my niece.' She is particularly attached to a grand-niece whom she also helped to bring up, having been very close to the brother, now dead, whose descendant this grand-niece was.

Miss Nash, 86 and another spinster, actually lives with a niece as well as a sister.

> Miss Nash shares with her 84-year-old widowed sister, Jane, and her niece Ethel, aged 42. She has been with Ethel for eighteen years, since Ethel's mother died. Jane joined them four years ago when *her* husband died. Ethel gets up at five every morning to do the heavy work of the house before she goes to her work as a typist. Miss Nash gets up too at that early hour and totters after Ethel through the different rooms. Jane does the cooking.

The other 14 single people were not living with siblings, and yet their behaviour underlined again the importance for spinsters of the relationship with other sisters. One of them was, for example, living with a niece, the daughter of a sister who had been very close till her death; one was with a grand-niece, again the descendant of a favourite sister; and a third was with a cousin. Another five were living with friends, all of them women friends who were treated very much as sisters.

> When Miss Knowles' mother died thirty years ago she invited a spinster friend of hers, Miss Spark, who worked in the same office, to come and live with her. They retired from work at about the same time. Miss Spark does most of the cooking and buying while Miss Knowles does the gardening and most of the housework. Miss Knowles said that she had that afternoon been 'spraying the roses because of the blackfly'. Miss Spark said, 'I mother her if she's ill. If one of us is ill the other will look after her. It's not that we wouldn't take help from anybody else or anything like that—it's just that we don't need it.'

But there were still six single people who lived alone. They all saw a great deal of their siblings if they had any. In fact, one of the striking things, in Woodford as in the East End, is how single people generally make up for the absence of other relationships by seeing more of their brothers and sisters. This is shown in Table VI to be true not only of old people but of those below pension age as well. Single people see their brothers and sisters much more often than do those who are, or have been, married.

TABLE VI

MARITAL STATUS AND LAST CONTACT WITH A SIBLING—
PEOPLE BELOW AND ABOVE PENSION AGE

(General sample—people with at least one sibling)

	Below pension age		Above pension age	
	Single	Married, Widowed and Divorced	Single	Married, Widowed and Divorced
Seen in previous 24 hours	65%	18%	43%	6%
Seen earlier in previous week ..	17%	25%	19%	18%
Not seen in previous week ..	18%	57%	38%	76%
Total %	100%	100%	100%	100%
Number ..	100	563	21	118

Miss Herson was one of the single people in the old age sample who saw a sister frequently although living alone. Until twelve years earlier she had been living with her younger sister Sarah, until Sarah got married, and since then she had visited her regularly every week, usually staying for a night or two.

'Yesterday I was staying over in Wimbledon with Sarah who lives there. I went over for dinner and after dinner I went with her to a church meeting, and at about four o'clock the meeting packed up and I went to the school to collect my little niece. Then I looked after my niece for the whole evening. Sarah went

54

out with her husband visiting friends of hers. Early this morning
I came back here by the tube. I'm very handy for the family, for
baby-sitting or anything like that—I'm useful to them because I
haven't got any family of my own to look after.'

Not all were as lucky as Miss Herson. Indeed one spinster,
Miss Spink, had no relatives at all, and no friends either.

Miss Spink is a retired schoolteacher aged 77, who lives at Woodford Wells. She suffers from rheumatism and has 'to go up the
stairs one at a time like a baby'. She lives alone in the home she
lived in as a child. 'My mother lived here before me', she said,
'and when she died I just carried on.' She was an only child and
she has no relatives, except 'some distant ones on my father's
side but I've lost contact with them'. She has few visitors—'The
Vicar comes about once a month, and the doctor about once
every six weeks—that's all.' She belongs to no clubs and goes
to church 'two or three times a year'.

But Miss Spink was the exception. The other single people
were not solitary. As we have seen, if they did not live with
siblings or other relatives, they made up for this either by
making a home with a friend, or by frequent contact with
their kin.

Widows without children

The other main group liable to isolation are the widowed
men and women who have no children.[1] They are that much
worse off than childless *married* people, who at least have each
other. In the old age sample there were ten people in this
state, of whom eight were widows and two widowers. Three
of the women were living with sisters. Mrs. Popham had
asked her unmarried sister to come and stay with her during
her husband's last illness; they have been together ever since.
She expressed herself very content, her only unsatisfied needs

[1] There were 55 widows and 14 widowers in the general sample; by coincidence, 55
were over, 14 under, pension age. Of the 14 younger ones, only one was living
alone, and she had her mother, also a widow, living within five minutes' walk.
All but three of the 14 had seen either their parents or a married child of their own
at some time in the previous week.

being 'a few friends and £750 a year'. Another widow was joined by her unmarried sister, who was not much help. 'She thinks she does her share of the work, but she doesn't really do much at all. She spends a whole morning polishing up the grate.' Mrs. Bagley's husband was killed at Mons in 1914, just after they were married. For many years after that Mrs. Bagley looked after her widowed father, until when he died she was invited to live with her married sister in Woodford. With their money combined they bought a large house with plenty of room for all. Mrs. Bagley makes a great fuss of her nephew, who still lives at home.

Of the seven widows not with sisters, the circumstances of the four with friends were much like those just described. The remaining three widows were living entirely alone, and about this all of them were unhappy, although they did see friends and relatives on occasion. One old woman, whose daughter had died, drew her consolation from the two grandsons she visited every Sunday afternoon; she complained, 'If people knew what it would be like when they reached my age, they wouldn't bother to go on living.' Another missed very much having someone in the house because she wasn't too firm on her feet and had to inch herself downstairs backwards; she couldn't depend on her arms to hold her if she should slip. An old widower, a retired gardener, regretted that his relatives were scattered. 'They're split up pretty tidy,' he said.

Another measure of isolation

The conclusion from this seems to be that of the childless old people in the old age sample in Woodford only four were truly on their own. With the possible exception of Miss Spink, even they were not at all recluses. These findings seem to match those of the previous chapter. But we ought, if we can, to test the extent of isolation in Woodford in other ways. An alternative means of measuring it, one which Townsend adopted in his survey in Bethnal Green, is to include everybody, whether or not they are married or have children, and whoever they live with, and attempt to give them a total 'score' according to the number of 'contacts' they have with other people during the week. We were able to collect, in interviewing the old age sample, comparable information to Townsend's for Bethnal Green and, in following him, have adopted the same arbitrary but workmanlike method of scoring 'contacts'. These include meetings with friends, visits to clubs, contacts at work and the like, as well as meetings with relatives inside and outside the same house. If a person lived in the same house as one other person, he was counted as having two contacts a day (14 a week) on that account alone, if he worked full-time that was counted as 20 contacts a week, and so on.[1]

Townsend regarded people as 'isolated' (again the measure is arbitrary, but serviceable) if they had three or less contacts a day, and found 10% of the 203 old people in the Bethnal Green old age sample in this plight. In Woodford, of the 210 people in the old age sample, the proportion, at 11%, is almost exactly the same.

Adaptability of the family

To sum up, most people are not solitary. Old people without children are on the whole no more isolated or neglected than those with them. The main reason is that the family, as adaptable in the suburb as in the city, is efficient at providing substitutes for its missing parts. In our earlier book we commented on the aptness of an eldest daughter to assume some of the functions of her mother, either as a 'little mother' during her own childhood or as the link with all her siblings after her mother was dead. The grandmother herself, in her role of Mum, could be regarded as in some sort a substitute for the husband who, in East London, at one time failed to give his wife the support she required. Townsend too showed how often when the inner family circle was incomplete or was broken by death or removal, a substitute was called in—grandparents instead of parents, sons of widows

[1] Fuller details are given in Townsend, P. B., op. cit., pp. 166–8.

instead of husbands, and only children instead of the other children. The same process is at work in the suburb. Examples are:

> Single people turn to siblings and form with them a version of a 'family of marriage'—Miss Beale, Miss Ley and Miss Nash provide examples of this.
>
> Childless people treat nieces and nephews as children, and grand-nieces and -nephews as grand-children—Miss Ley or Mrs. Bagley being illustrations.
>
> Single people without relatives make a kind of 'family' with single friends as 'quasi-siblings'—like Miss Knowles.

Almost everyone succeeds, somehow or other, in surrounding himself with a family or its atmosphere. Why people *need* a family of some kind, especially in later life, is obvious. What is less clear is why the relatives who are thus sought after should respond. Often, of course, the arrangement is of mutual benefit—the spinster sisters or friends both need each other. Where this is not so, the relatives—nephews and nieces and others—seem to feel a sense of obligation, perhaps weaker than that of children to their parents, but at least akin to it. Mr. Loder's niece, with whom he lives, confided, 'He's an awful nuisance sometimes, but I *can't* turn him out, can I? After all, he's my father's brother and there's no one else he could go to.'

The cares of ageing

We can summarize the conclusion of these two chapters on old people by saying that, despite the kinship differences in the two districts, the family is as much a support to its aged members in the suburb as in the East End. But it would be misleading to leave the subject of old people's care without recalling, however briefly, some of the less happy aspects of old age. For one thing, we have said that around 10% of old people in both districts could be described as 'isolated'. This is a minority, but in these two districts alone it amounts to well over 1,500 people, and if the proportions apply nationally, to something like 700,000 of the old people in Great

Britain. What is more, this leaves out the old people in institutions (estimated at some 3% of the people of pension age in Great Britain), who were excluded altogether from our samples of people in *private* households. There is clearly an immense task for the formal social services, health, housing and welfare, to discharge if they are to take care of the minority who are not cared for by their families—immense because the minority is so substantial.

Even those old people who are living with or near their relatives may have their troubles. The previous chapter discussed the problems that sometimes arise between the generations when a home is shared, and sisters or other relatives likewise do not necessarily get on all that smoothly with each other. Then, for some, there is the loneliness of widowhood; people often miss their partner even when they are living in the thick of the family. 'My daughter pops up all the time from the shop downstairs', said one widow, 'But I feel lonely for my husband. I do miss him.' Another widow, also sharing a house with a married daughter, said, 'When you lose your partner you lose all interest in things. Of the 89 widowed people in the old age sample, 55% said they were 'often' or 'sometimes' lonely, against 20% of the 25 single and 16% of the 96 married people. That sense of loss is something against which children and other kin cannot provide protection.

Finally, relatives may be able to ease, but they cannot remove, the pain and depression caused by the infirmity or ill-health that eventually overtakes most old people. 'I can't get around as I used to', as one old woman explained, 'It's like the animals. You've only got to watch them to see what happens.' 'I just can't seem to walk any more, the ground seems to come up', remarked an 81-year-old widow who is living with one of her children, 'If only the doctor would give me some tablets. There's only one thing I want and that's a little happiness.' Mr. Mitson, aged 83 and married, said, 'I get pneumonia every winter. I can't dig the garden any more or mow the grass, I get so horribly breathless. I feel so frustrated.' 'Life isn't really much fun when you get old,' declared Mr. Collis.

These are the kind of burdens most old people cannot escape. But all are lighter when there are children or other relatives close by to give a hand. Despite the reservations, the main conclusion of these two chapters stands. Kinship in the suburb brings crucial aid not so much to young married couples as to old people—those without children of their own hardly less than those with. 'People may have less to do with each other on the social side than they used to in the past', as Mrs. Connelly put it, 'but they still stick together if someone's in trouble.'

VI

MOTHERS AND DAUGHTERS

EVEN in the suburb, the wider family organizes care
and support for those in need. In some, at least, of its
functions it is similar to its counterpart in the East End.
But is it organized in a similar way? In Bethnal Green the
kinship system was built around the close tie between
mother and daughter—it was the axis of the local kinship
structure. Is it the same in the suburb?

This is not one question but two. The first is whether in
Woodford the children's tie is more with the mother than the
father. The second is whether the parental tie is more with
daughters than sons. We shall discuss each of these questions
in turn.

Fathers and mothers

The grandmother, or 'Mum', as she was universally called,
was certainly the dominant figure in Bethnal Green. The
chief organizer of family parties or of aid, she was something
of a matriarchal figure. The local family group, linked together through her bond with her married daughters, was
united on her hearth. 'The family rendezvous' was how one
woman described her mother's home. 'Mum's is the central
depot in this family', said a respectful dustman of his mother-
in-law.

The fathers, particularly the older ones, were often excluded from this family circle. Townsend found that the
more women shared their daily lives with daughters, the less
they did with husbands. In many ways the lives of father and
mother were separate. There was a sharp financial division

61

between the sexes; women whose husbands were still at work received a fixed, often barely adequate, 'wage' from them and did not know how much they earned. The man lived his own life, had his own interests and friends, outside the women's world of the extended family.[1]

We did, however, find little evidence of the same kind of segregation between the *younger* Bethnal Green couples. Patterns are changing and the old marital relationship is giving way to one based more on 'partnership'. But at the time of our surveys in Bethnal Green, the position of the old men was certainly unenviable, especially after retirement. While he was still at work he had his status as a bread-winner and a useful member of the community, he had his work-mates, he had money in his pocket. After retirement, which was almost always forced on him by ill-health or the decree of his employer, he became a rather pathetic figure, as Townsend makes plain. He felt he had lost his 'prestige and standing in both locality and family'.[2]

Old men in Woodford

The working-class father in Woodford shares some of the same problems on retirement. His income falls sharply. Table VII refers to the personal incomes of the single and widowed men in the old age sample and the joint incomes of the married men with their wives and the married women with their husbands. The date is 1957, when the interviews with this sample were carried out.

Working-class people get less money both in work and in retirement. Many middle-class people suffer a sharp drop too, but their income does not fall to such a low level mainly because more of them get a pension from their firm and are thus not so dependent upon the State. A quarter of working-class retired men in the Woodford old age sample, but three-quarters of middle-class, receive some form of pen-

1 Townsend, P. B., op. cit., pp. 67–72.
2 Ibid., p. 147.

Table VII

Average Weekly Income of People Working and Retired from Full-time Work, according to Social Class

(Old age sample—widows and single women excluded)

	Middle Class		Working Class	
	Average weekly income	*Number*	*Average weekly income*	*Number*
Working full-time	£19 12s.	13	£10 14s.	24
Retired from full-time work ..	£9 10s.	41	£4 7s.	27

sion from their employer. 'I get a pension from my firm', said a former accountant, 'which of course puts me on easy street. We can manage quite comfortably.' A bank manager told us that he got a pension two-thirds of his final salary. 'If you got £1,500, you get £1,000. The drop isn't really very serious, because that £500 was taxed at 8s. 6d. in the pound. You don't have to travel up to work, so you're not more than about two or three hundred pounds down.'

'Since my husband retired', said the wife of a former insurance manager, 'we haven't really altered our standard of living much. It's just that we don't save any more, that, and adjusting, rather than actually going without. In the matter of food we're never wasteful, and we don't have all the expensive things at the same time. If we're having fried egg for breakfast *with* bacon or tomatoes, we have the small, cheaper eggs. We only have the large if we're having boiled.' Their milk bill—for three—is usually 8s. 6d. a week. The wine bill is £6 a month—'cider and squash every week, a Triple Crown port and a Bristol Cream

63

sherry every month—and we've always got a bottle of good whisky in the house'.

Working-class husbands seldom had the same satisfaction. Their homes were not supported on a substantial retirement income provided from their past efforts. To put it another way, some retired manual workers in Woodford shared with those in Bethnal Green the feeling that they had lost their status along with their job and the income it provided. They felt that they had no real place in the home, that they were useless and 'in the way'. 'What's the good of mooching around here all the time?' asked Mr. Garner, a retired labourer, 'I see enough of the wife without sitting here all day. I wish I was still at work.' 'He just sits around here all day since he gave up work,' said Mrs. Everard of her husband, a former toolmaker, 'He gets in my way more than anything.'

But these were exceptions, and though financially the working-class retired men in Woodford are worse off than the middle-class, in other important ways they are more like them than like the manual workers of Bethnal Green. On the whole, even working-class fathers in Woodford do not feel excluded from the home. On the contrary, their relationship with their wives is a close one. 'Partnership' has gone further in Woodford than in the East End, among the older married couples as among the younger. Woodford fathers and mothers more often own their homes and have gardens to tend, and the interest in the house and garden is something the couples hold in common.

The old people of Woodford, in all classes, seem altogether to have a more companionate conception of marriage—we have reported earlier that the older men regularly helped their wives with housework in over four-fifths of the couples in the Woodford old age sample, against less than half in Bethnal Green.[1] This co-operation is specially evident in retirement. Mr. Harding, a retired bank clerk, helps his wife with the week-end shopping every Friday afternoon, does

[1] See Chapter II, p. 22.

some of the washing and makes the bed, because she is not strong enough to turn the mattress. 'We share the gardening', he says, 'I dig and she does the planting.' Mr. Browning helps his wife with the polishing every morning and 'always takes the laundry round to the shop'. 'We go fifty-fifty in all the jobs in the house,' said another retired man, Mr. Britland. 'My husband', said Mrs. Marston, 'does all the heavy cleaning and most of the shopping. I do the cooking and ironing and most of the washing, but he wrings it out for me. We both do the garden but he does most.' Mr. Stockman, a retired Civil Servant, also takes great pride in his garden, with its lily pond and goldfish, its lawn and stone statues; he and his wife do the housework together, and in the afternoons and evenings play cards, read to each other and do crosswords together. Generally, the older Woodford parents share each other's lives in this sort of way.

This 'partnership' of father and mother is obviously encouraged by the kinship patterns of the suburb. In Bethnal Green, daughters are nearby from their wedding day on, and the mother has their company to fill her life, their needs to occupy her energies. In a suburb like Woodford, children are not present throughout life, though they may be in the parents' later years. Middle-aged mothers and fathers, with their children off the scene, are much more likely than in Bethnal Green to lead shared lives, to develop common interests, to deepen their attachment to each other.

But this closer bond between father and mother, in its turn, affects the kinship system. If the parents are together then we can expect their children to see as much of one as the other, rather than seeing *mothers* more frequently, as in the East End. Where kinship is a day-to-day affair, with daughters calling in once or twice every day, the fathers will often be left out. Where, as in the suburb, the meetings between parents and children are more often weekly or fortnightly, both parents are likely to be on the scene. The visits are often at the week-end and usually the children go to the parent's home—over two-thirds of mothers, for example, had last been seen by their married children in their own home. 'We nearly always go round to them', as Mrs. Miles said about her parents. 'Whether it's his parents or mine,' said Mrs. Baxter, 'we usually visit them. They don't come here so much.'

So, when son or daughter calls at the parental home, father is probably there as well as mother—painting the stairs, perhaps, or planting lettuces in the garden, or cleaning up the bedroom. This is true whether he has retired or not. If he has not, the visits will usually be at times when he is not working. If he is older and has retired, the children, as we showed in Chapter IV, are likely to visit more often—as often as in the East End—but by then he too will be at home more of the time.

All this suggests that fathers in Woodford may be seen almost as often as mothers. This is so; Table VIII shows it.

TABLE VIII

CONTACTS WITH MOTHERS AND FATHERS

(General sample—married people with mother/father alive)

	Mothers	Fathers
Seen in previous 24 hours ..	30%	25%
Seen earlier in previous week ..	33%	34%
Not seen in previous week ..	37%	41%
Total %	100%	100%
Number	346	234

Mothers and fathers are seen about as frequently as each other because they are together. But if one is dead they obviously cannot be together and, as the numbers in Table VIII indicate, there are many more mothers alive than fathers. The proportions in the table, which are of mothers and fathers

66

seen *out of those who were alive*, conceal the fact that, in practice, just because women usually outlive their husbands, they actually do figure more in the lives of their children. Among the 795 married people in the general sample as a whole—irrespective of whether their parents were alive—28% had seen mothers in the previous week, against 17% who had seen fathers. The differential death rates for older men and women have important implications for parent-child relationships—a fact, incidentally, whose importance we did not sufficiently recognize in the Bethnal Green studies.

Sons and daughters

Widows apart, there is no marked difference in people's contacts with mothers as against fathers. That is the conclusion so far, from looking at the parents. Now we turn to the children, comparing sons and daughters in their relationships with their parents. The first question is where the children live. In the East End, daughters live with or near their parents after marriage more often than sons—or, in other words, couples live with or near the wife's parents more often than the husband's. Residence, as the anthropologists would put it, is matrilocal.

Is it like this in Woodford? Let us look first at people living *with* parents; do couples in the suburb more often live with the wife's parents or the husband's? Of the 193 married women in the general sample with one or both parents alive, 13% lived in the same house with them, against 5% of the 202 married men. So, in sharing the house, residence *is* matrilocal[1] here as in the East End. We talked in an earlier chapter about parents joining their children with advancing age or upon the death of a spouse. Now we can see that it is predominantly their *daughters* they join.

---

[1] Strictly speaking, this is not the correct term. In an Appendix to *Family and Kinship in East London* we discussed the various meanings of this, among other kinship terms (p. 203). There is a further difficulty in Woodford, since, as Chapter IV showed, what happens more often is not that the children move to live with or near one set of *parents* after marriage, but rather that the parents move in old age to live with or near their daughters or sons.

People in both places gave much the same sort of reasons for preferring to share with the wife's parents—or sharing with their daughters, to look at it from the viewpoint of the older generation. As some of the older women expressed it, mothers and daughters can get along in the same house because they have grown up together and are used to each other's ways. Between mother and daughter-in-law, on the other hand, there is usually potential or actual rivalry. There are often, we saw earlier, tensions between the generations sharing a house, and most people seemed to feel that these difficulties were intensified when one woman was not the child of the other. Mrs. Connelly, a widow living with her only son, explained how difficult it was:

'After my husband died', she said, 'I was on my own. Directly my daughter-in-law knew, she said, "You must come to us". I thought that was very nice, coming from a daughter-in-law. We get on very well together, but I have to be careful. If you're living with a daughter-in-law you must never, never take your son's part. You must never seem to be siding with him against your daughter-in-law, and you must never tell her what he likes and what he doesn't. You must leave her to find out about that sort of thing for herself.'

Mrs. Ripley had tried living with her son and his wife but had since moved away to live alone. 'My daughter-in-law is a wonderful girl,' she said, 'but her ways are not my ways.' 'If you are cooking or something', explained Mrs. Temperley, 'you can't seem to get on with your daughter-in-law's methods. It's different with your own daughter—her way is more like your own way.'

It is easy to see why the parents might prefer to live in the same house as their daughter rather than their son. But what about those not living in the same house as children—do they live *nearer* daughters or sons? Table IX shows, according to the sex of the informants, just where their parents live. Outside the house shared by the two generations, there is not at all the same trend. The other variations in the table are

68

TABLE IX

PROXIMITY OF PARENTS TO MARRIED MEN AND WOMEN
(General sample—married men and women with at least one
parent alive)

Parents' Residence	Men	Women
Same house	5%	13%
Within five minutes' walk ..	9%	6%
Elsewhere in Woodford	16%	14%
Outside Woodford	70%	67%
Total %	100%	100%
Number	201	193

slight.[1] In other words, matrilocality in Woodford only applies to couples who live *with* the wife's parents.

Daughters not sharing a home with parents may live no nearer than sons; the crucial question is whether they see them more. In answering this, it is necessary to take distance into account. If the parents live more than twenty miles away, for instance, they are seen as much by sons as by daughters. But within a radius of twenty miles there was an evident difference—67% of the 136 sons, against 81% of the 104 daughters, seeing their mothers in the previous week. It is much the same with fathers. Daughters, in other words, not only *live* with parents more often than sons; they also see them more often when they live apart, at least when they are within reasonable visiting distance.

Parents-in-law and grandmothers

This has a number of important consequences for the kinship system. For one thing, it affects people's relationships

[1] As a check we examined the relationships from the angle of the *parents*, seeing whether their sons, as a whole, lived nearer than their daughters. Again, many more daughters than sons were in the same house, but otherwise there were no marked differences between the sexes.

with their parents-in-law. If a couple live with the wife's parents, then the husband automatically sees his parents-in-law more than his own parents. If they do not live together, the couple will usually go together on visits and again will see his wife's parents more than she sees his. Of the 127 married men in the general sample with a father-in-law alive, for example, 52% had seen him in the previous week; of the 95 married women with a father-in-law, 37% had seen him in the same period. 'We go over to his parents spasmodically', said Mrs. Archer, 'We see mine more often.'

In the same way, the grandchildren see their mother's parents—their maternal grandparents—more than their father's. We asked the people in the old age sample how often, on average, they saw each of their grandchildren. As many as 52% of the 277 daughters' children, against 30% of the 291 sons' children, were seen once a week or more. As one grandmother put it, 'With your daughter's children you feel it's more like your *own* children than your son's are.'

Grandparents, particularly grandmothers, though they help with the daily round less often than in the East End, do give some assistance in the care of their grandchildren. Mrs. Hartley is one; her daughter works as a shorthand-typist. She can carry on full-time because during the school holidays Mrs. Hartley looks after her granddaughter during the daytime. Mrs. Anderson is another who helps. She told us:

'I'm going to look after a grandchild on Saturday, when I'm over at my daughter's. I've often sat in for them. That's what grandmothers are for, aren't they? Their son is a very nice little boy, he calls me Mammy.'

Mrs. Thomas is a third. She and her husband do not live so near, but they have their grandchildren to stay with them.

'We have the grandchildren to stay for a week at a time. We put them on camp beds in the sitting-room. They love it—they call it the "Green Room", because of the furnishings, you know.'

Altogether nearly half the people in the old age sample who

had grandchildren regularly give them pocket money or gifts in kind:

> 'We give them money or some little thing whenever they call. You wouldn't be proper grandparents if you didn't do that—that's what they come for. I knit things for all of them. It's part of your life, isn't it?'

> 'I generally give Elizabeth something. I say "There's something for your piggy-wiggy". That's her little safe. We know when she's coming and we have some sweets for her.'

> 'We give the grandchildren two shillings a week each—half to save—half to spend. And we're always buying them sweets and things. To me it's like living all over again when you've got grandchildren.'

> 'Do we see the grandson? That's all we go there for. We don't give him money—he's only four—but we wouldn't be grandparents if we didn't take him something every week.'

So the grandparents are not unfamiliar or shadowy figures in the suburb. They are known and usually loved—though one child interrupted her mother at an interview to say, 'We all hate it when Granny comes. It's terrible. We're so glad when she goes home.' More characteristic was the little girl who told her grandmother, 'Don't die yet, will you Granny? I love you so much and I want you to come to my wedding.' Feelings aside, most of the grandparents make a point of seeing their grandchildren regularly, and many help out on their behalf.

Help for the parents

But help *from* the older generation is less common in Woodford than help *to* them. The real contrast with the East End is that there the generations are side by side throughout life, and at every stage kinship provides aid and support—for the expectant wife no less than the middle-aged mother struck down by illness, for the mother with young children no less than the aged widow. In the suburb, help is much more one-way, the younger couple on the whole receiving much less than, at the crucial stage, they give to parents who are widowed, infirm or ailing. The fact is that, despite the examples we have given of grandparents' generosity to grandchildren, they are in Woodford less likely to be giving substantial help than seeking it.

There are, in other words, two crucial stages in adult life, which correspond to those distinguished in earlier chapters. From the parents' point of view, these two stages are:

> *In middle age*, when they have young married children, they live farther away from them than in the East End, see less of them, and do less to help them.
> *In old age*, they move with or near children, see them more often than before, and receive help *from* them.

In this second stage, the parents live with daughters more than sons and see them more frequently if they do not live with them. Whether they live with them or not, the help they receive comes much more often from daughters than from sons. This reliance on daughters is shown when help in illness is considered. Table X includes people who do not live with children as well as those who do.

The dependence on daughters is very striking in both places. We also asked whom people would turn to in a future illness. In Woodford, of the 116 people in the old age sample with at least one daughter alive, 64, or 55%, named a daughter. In Bethnal Green, of the 144 with at least one daughter, 128, or 89%, said they would turn to a daughter. Daughters, it seems, are even more the standby in the East End. But the vital part they played was also plain enough in the suburb, as the interviews made clear:

> 'If I'm on the poorly side my daughter Rosie comes across. She lives just over the road. My two daughters at Walthamstow, they come every week and give me a good clean up.'

> 'If I don't feel too good, Joan comes over and takes my washing and brings it back all ironed.'

> 'My daughter had me this summer after I came out of hospital. I wanted to come home, but it was doctor's orders, I'd got to go

TABLE X

SOURCE OF HELP IN ILLNESS

(Woodford and Bethnal Green Old Age Samples—old people experiencing recent illness)*

	Woodford	Bethnal Green
Husband or wife	32%	31%
Daughter	34%	41%
Other relative	23%	22%
Other person	8%	4%
No help	3%	2%
Total %	100%	100%
Number	140	101

* The comparison is not exact. In Bethnal Green the period was confined to the last two years, in Woodford to the last five.

and stay with my daughter. She nursed me for two weeks—nobody in to help, no, and then I came back here on my own. If I wasn't very well anytime, I'd always turn to my daughter.'

Daughters also gave a great deal of help on more ordinary occasions. When we considered who helped the old people with various household tasks—shopping, cooking, cleaning and washing—daughters emerged as more important in the household economy than any other relatives.[1] Again, many examples were given in the interviews of daughters helping parents who were infirm:

When asked whether she ever called on the District Nurse, Mrs. Arkwright pointed to her daughter and said, 'That's my nurse. She does everything she can for me. If I'm worried about anything or in any trouble or I need anything, it's always to her I fly, and she always puts me right.'

'My husband says I'm rough,' Mrs. Rees explained, 'so Peggy

[1] See Appendix 4, Table XLVI.

does things for him, now he's so weak. She washes him and shaves him, cuts his hair and everything.'

'I wash her hair and set it for her, and then I always bath her', said one daughter of her mother, 'She's nervous of getting into the bath alone—she's afraid she'll never be able to get out again, so I'm always there with her.'

A mother-daughter bond?

How are we to sum up? Daughters live with parents more often, see more of them, and generally play a bigger part than sons, especially in the care they provide. But, if we leave aside the mother-daughter unions that follow from older women outliving their husbands, there is little evidence that daughters have very much more to do with mothers than with fathers. If we measure by the frequency of contact, in other words, the tie in the suburb seems to be between the daughter and *both* parents, rather than with the mother alone. Yet it was clear to us from the interviews we had with people in both generations that there is some special emotional bond between mother and daughter.

The younger women often spoke about it, even those who lived at a distance from their mother or whose mother was dead. Mrs. Holmes, whose parents live in Reading, explained that she would not think of emigrating; 'I couldn't leave my parents. I'm very fond of my mother and if I did go away I might never see her again.' 'If I was in a spot, I would turn to her for help,' she added, 'Your mother's the most natural person to turn to.' Mrs. Day lamented, 'I do long for somebody of my own, especially in times of trouble. I've got no mother or sisters, you see.' Mrs. Bentley tried to explain the tie: 'A daughter alters when she gets married and has children of her own. She seems to feel closer to her mother then than before. They understand each other more.' 'I can't really explain it', said Mrs. Green, 'But there does seem to be a specially close feeling between a mother and her daughter.'

The older women, too, sometimes spoke about the relationship. 'There's nobody like a daughter,' said Mrs. Yale. Mrs. Lacey told us, 'My sons have all been very good to me, but a daughter's a daughter after all and there's a world of difference.' 'My daughter', said Mrs. Beaver, 'is everything to me. I should be nowhere without her.' Mrs. Sankey did not have a daughter, and knew how much this mattered. 'Oh, I do wish I'd had a daughter. I've got good sons but it's not the same as a daughter.' Mrs. Broadbent, talking about her youngest daughter, said, 'She's been such a good girl to me. Of course I've had her home longer than the others and more recently. She was my baby and we're very close to each other.'

We cannot but take note of these opinions, unsubstantiated though they are by much statistical evidence. Our conclusion is that the bond between the two women is not only a reality, but an essential feature of kinship in Woodford as in Bethnal Green. The daughters *see* their fathers as much as mothers in the suburb for the simple reason, as we have shown earlier in this chapter, that the older parents are themselves together more. Fathers are seen mainly because they are *with* mothers.

This view that there is some special attachment between the women seems to be supported when we look at relationships with siblings. Women see their sisters more than their brothers and more than men see either brothers or sisters.[1] 'I don't know why it is', said Mrs. Eton, 'but I somehow feel more attached to my sister than my brothers.' People do not see their siblings anything like as often as they see their parents, of course, but it looks as if, in Woodford as in the East End, there is a somewhat similar (though less intense) tie between sister and sister as between mother and daughter. The strongest links are between women in both districts.

And yet, in other ways, Woodford is not at all the same. The mother is nothing like the dominating East End Mum. Her authority is much more restricted and, if she goes to live with her daughter, she may even find herself in a rather subordinate position. Above all, her daughter matters less to the mother as long as her own husband is alive, because the older

[3] See Appendix 4, Table XLVII.

parents share so much of their lives with each other. Here lies the big difference between the two districts. In the one, mothers and daughters are each other's constant companions and helpmates. In the other, the same bond is still there, in affection and in the care and support that daughters give their mothers—and, to a lesser extent, their fathers—in their advancing years. But it is by and large less important in Woodford because the relationship of husband and wife matters more.

VII

CLASS AND FAMILY VISITING

So far in this book we have been discussing social class more implicitly than explicitly. The emphasis has been on the contrast between the districts. The one district is working-class and the other is not, and so the contrast between the places which has engaged our attention is to some extent also a contrast between classes. But to what extent? We do not know how far such differences in family behaviour as we have found are connected with other features of the two communities besides class. The districts vary in other ways too—for instance, in the length of time for which people have lived in them. All we can be fairly sure of is that the family differences are due, in some part, to class.

We are now going to do what we have for the sake of exposition avoided doing up to now, and that is observe the influence of class on family in another, more direct way, by comparing the classes within Woodford. Sometimes we may in the foregoing chapters have given the impression that Woodford is almost entirely middle-class. If so it was not intentional. As we said in the Introduction and in Chapter I, manual workers (or the 'working class') constitute a sizeable part of the population. There are quite enough of them to compare with the non-manual (or 'middle-class') residents of the district.

The influence of class upon membership of formal organizations and upon friendships is examined in the following three chapters. Here our concern is still with the family, and the first question is once again about residence. Do working-class people live nearer to their parents? The answer is given

77

in Table XI, which also gives the Bethnal Green figures for comparison.

TABLE XI

PARENTS' RESIDENCE, ACCORDING TO DISTRICT AND SOCIAL CLASS OF INFORMANT

(General samples—married people with at least one parent alive)

Parents' Residence	Woodford		Bethnal Green
	Middle-Class	Working-Class	
Same dwelling	8%	11%	12%
Within five minutes' walk	6%	10%	29%
Elsewhere in borough	12%	21%	13%
Outside borough ..	74%	58%	46%
Total %	100%	100%	100%
Number	242	152	369

The answer is clear—in Woodford working-class people do, by and large, live closer to their parents. We know from Chapter III that a similar kind of comparison can be made between the districts—Bethnal Greeners also live closer to their parents. Table XI also shows that the proportion of Bethnal Greeners living close to their parents is higher than the proportion of working-class people doing so in Woodford. Altogether 26% of Woodford's middle class, 42% of Woodford's working class, and 54% of Bethnal Green's population have parents in the same borough. It seems that as far as residence is concerned there is a kind of 'kinship continuum' from Woodford's middle class, through Woodford's working class, to Bethnal Green.[1]

[1] Further tables comparing (a) the two districts and (b) the classes inside Woodford are set out in Appendix 4.

Class and Family Visiting

The Woodford working class more often have relatives at hand. Does it follow that they also see more of them than their middle-class neighbours do? The answer in general terms is that class has rather less effect on the amount of contact within families than it does upon residence.[2] One of the main reasons is obvious. Since middle-class people more often have cars, even though they live farther away, distance does not matter as much to them. This can be illustrated by what happens with brothers and sisters. People in the general sample whose nearest sibling lived right outside Woodford were more likely to have seen him or her if they had a car. Thirty-two per cent of the 242 people with a car had done so in the previous week, against 23% of the 271 without. Mr. Devon, a schoolteacher, is one man who uses his car regularly for this purpose; he drives an elderly sister to church at Barking every Sunday and on the way back he picks up his brother and brings him back to dinner. Mr. Prior, a bank manager, explained what he does: 'I go over to Harringay to pick up my mother for the week-end occasionally. I drop her back there on my way to work on Monday morning.'

Middle-class people more often have room in their homes for relatives to stay for a week-end or a fortnight. As a result they more often spend part of their annual holidays at a relative's home. 'We go and stay with my father in Lincolnshire every summer,' said Mrs. Hammond. What is more, middle-class people more often have telephones, and so are able to maintain contact in this way, even if they do not meet. 'We ring my parents up every month to see how they are,' said a Civil Servant's wife. 'I've got a sister in Ealing', the wife of a company secretary told us, 'I'm always talking to her on the phone.' An accountant's wife said, 'I speak to all my sisters at least once a week on the telephone.'

Finally, they write more. A schoolteacher's wife who writes about ten letters a week, including some to relatives in Australia and New Zealand, explained, 'I don't see them very often, but if you write a letter you feel you're talking to them.'

[2] For further evidence see Tables XLII to XLV, in Appendix 4.

The wife of a works manager said, 'We keep in touch with the family by letter.' It was, ironically enough, a postman's wife who expressed a common working-class view—'I don't like writing letters, so I don't write to nobody and nobody writes to me.' A warehouseman said, 'If I don't see my brothers and sisters, that's that. We don't write to each other.' Cars, telephones and letters are all means by which middle-class people can straddle the distance they have interposed between themselves and their relatives. With these technical aids, the middle-class people of Woodford keep in touch with relatives almost as much as working-class people do, although they do not live as close.

The conclusion so far is that there is a difference between the classes in Woodford, of the same kind as there is between the districts. But we have also seen that the working class of Woodford is placed somewhere between the two extremes, on the whole being rather more similar to the local middle class than to Bethnal Green. It seems that if anything the influence of the district they live in is stronger than the influence of occupation. This conclusion is, as we have seen, partly the result not of what working-class people are like, but of what middle-class people do to overcome distance. But this is not the whole story.

The other explanation is that, while the working class of Bethnal Green live in a district to all intents and purposes one-class, and that their own, the working class of Woodford do not. They live in an area dominated by the middle class. Middle-class behaviour, middle-class attitudes, middle-class houses surround them. And, of course, in material standards, the lives of many of them *are* more like those of the middle classes. Over a third of working-class householders of Woodford own their own houses, for example, whereas hardly any Bethnal Greeners do. Often, too, they have moved into Woodford in order to get a house and the other necessities of middle-class life. Only 15% of Woodford working-class people are natives of the place; many of the others, as we said in Chapter I, have moved in from the East End itself, or from other predominantly working-class East London districts like East Ham, Leyton or Walthamstow, and the move out has for them been a move 'up' as well. In one way or another, it seems to us, the working-class people of Woodford are, despite having the same kinds of manual occupations, more like their neighbours than like Bethnal Greeners. This is as true of kinship as it is of other things.

Occupational mobility

Woodford gave us an opportunity to inquire not only into the influence of being in one class rather than another, but also the influence of moving from one class to another. This was something we could not do in Bethnal Green because it consists almost entirely of people who have stayed in the working class. The ones who move out of the class also move out of the district. We tracked down some of the women who had migrated after they had attended a local grammar school, and our findings were reported very briefly in the previous book.[1] But this was an unsatisfactory study, and we welcomed a fuller chance to inquire whether, for example, the son of a plumber who becomes a university lecturer moves away from his parents in more than body. This seemed particularly worth doing because other sociologists have shown that occupational mobility is one of the crucial processes of industrial society.[2] Professor Glass and his colleagues at the London School of Economics have begun to measure the extent of occupational mobility in Britain in a systematic way and in the United States several writers have commented on the disruptive effects of mobility upon the extended family. Homans and Schneider said, for instance, that 'Upward mobile persons keep only shallow ties with members of their kindred if they keep them at all; downward mobile persons may be neglected by their kindred.'[3] Parsons

---

[1] *Family and Kinship in East London*, Chapter XI.
[2] Glass, D. V., *Social Mobility in Britain*. See also Douglas, J. W. B., and Blomfield, J. M., *Children under Five*, pp. 30–33.
[3] Schneider, D. M., and Homans, G. C., 'Kinship Terminology and the American Kinship System.'

said something similar in a celebrated sociological essay.[1]

The first question we asked was whether Woodford was different from Bethnal Green in having substantial numbers of people who had moved from one occupational group to another. We were quickly satisfied by the answer. More than a third of the people have moved up or down the scale compared to their fathers.[2] The proportion of men moving upwards is about the same as that which two leading American investigators, Lipset and Bendix,[3] have shown to obtain in most of the industrial countries of the world.

The second and main question was about the effect which this mobility had on the family. To answer it, many scores of statistical tabulations have been made. Some of the key tables are given in Appendix 3. Here we will only mention what seemed to us to be the main conclusion. This was that mobility affected men but not women. Table XII shows that sons who moved either upwards or downwards into another class saw less of their fathers than sons who remained in the same class as their fathers.

There were plenty of individual examples in the interviews to show that a minority of men believed that occupational advancement—their own or other people's—had weakened kinship relations. As might have been expected, it was seldom the people who *had* been successful themselves who talked about this, though Mr. Jenkins, a sales manager, did say, 'I wanted something different from my family. Their way of life wasn't my idea. I was always different from my brothers and sisters and I've never bothered to keep up with them.' For the most part those who spoke about it were those who felt that some of their more successful relatives were 'snobbish' and 'standoffish', particularly some working-class people with brothers in non-manual jobs. One example was a lorry-driver, most of whose brothers were in 'white-collar' jobs.

[1] Parsons, T., 'Revised Analytical Approach to the Theory of Social Stratification.'
[2] See Appendix 3 for an account of our methods of analysis.
[3] Lipset, S. M., and Bendix, R., *Social Mobility in Industrial Society.*

TABLE XII

CONTACT OF MEN WITH FATHERS, ACCORDING TO OCCUPATIONAL MOBILITY OF INFORMANT

(General sample—married men with fathers alive)

	Men	
	Mobile	*Not Mobile*
Fathers seen in previous 24 hours	13%	29%
Seen earlier in previous week ..	30%	37%
Not seen in previous week ..	57%	34%
Total %	100%	100%
Number	76	49

'I was the dunce in the family. The others have all done very well. I've a brother who lives at Upminster. He sends Christmas cards and telephones to find out how I am. But I never see him. I've a brother at Chadwell Heath. I never see him either. I've got along without them all these years and I can get along without them now.'

Another informant, a labourer, last saw his brother, a foreman, before the war, when he was unemployed and went to ask about getting a job. 'He told me, "Don't you ever come up here again showing me up". I haven't seen him since.' The same sort of thing seemed to apply with more remote relatives. A window-cleaner said that he had a nephew living in a nearby street in Wanstead. 'We don't see anything of them', his wife said, 'they think they're a bit above us.' One housewife said of her nephew and his wife, also living in the district, 'They're too uppish for me, or at least they think they are.'

Parents whose sons had moved up were inclined to complain in a general way about the younger generation. 'I think the young people of today are more selfish', said one woman whose only son had 'got on', 'We used to stick to our parents in the old days.' 'I don't think there's that love for the parents that there used to be', remarked the wife of a retired shop assistant who is similarly placed. A telephone engineer was another. One of his sons lives and works in Australia.

'I made things very different for my boys,' he said. 'Different to how I had it. But to tell you the truth, I sometimes wonder if I was wise. I mean, if Frank hadn't got on, he might have got married and settled down near here and then there'd have been grandchildren. Frank's brilliant, you see, and I encouraged him to take a scholarship to Cambridge. He got a first-class honours degree and became a top-level specialist in aeronautical engineering. The Government sent him to Australia on secret work and he's stayed on out there with an Australian firm. We don't write: I don't even know his address. He's like Greta thingummy—he wants to be alone. But there you are—I put him on his feet and he must go his own way.'

All the examples given are of men whose links with their relatives have been weakened by mobility. Although men predominate, we do not want to leave the impression that women were not affected at all by their daughters' marriages. A commercial traveller's wife was one who certainly was. She has three daughters, all married to men with professional or managerial jobs, and none of them would take their parents in. 'I do think', she said, 'that one of our children might have found room for us. The younger people haven't got any time for their parents these days.' But on the whole daughters did not figure as large in the accounts which we were given of the disrupting effects of mobility.

Why should fathers and sons be affected so by occupational mobility when mothers and daughters are not? The short answer is very simple—because whatever may happen to sons or sons-in-law, mothers and daughters continue to have the same principal job in life. When fathers and sons similarly have the same occupation, on farm or in family business of any kind, they have a similar bond,[1] but when they not only have different occupations but these carry different social status, for many of them the bond becomes a barrier. Men naturally judge each other according to the jobs they hold, and are liable to feel uneasy with any close relative who has in the worldly sense succeeded more than they have themselves. The examples we have given show what this discomfort can mean. But, as we say, women are not similarly divided. Daughter follows mother in her main occupations of child-rearing and housekeeping. They have the additional ties that daughters still usually learn the rudiments of each craft from their mothers, and that to some degree, however slight, they share those who are one woman's children and the other's grandchildren. The nature of these ties in Bethnal Green we explored in the earlier book, and we have noted their strength even on the shifting scene of the suburb in the previous chapter to this. Here we need only add that our finding on social mobility provides yet further confirmation of the elemental nature of the relationship. A mother ordinarily continues to see her daughter whether she is married to a man either higher or lower in the occupational scale. In most families this tie resists occupational changes whose more dire influence men cannot avoid. We recognize that on this subject our inquiry is only a beginning; the evidence is slight, and needs to be supplemented by much further work before one could be sure that what happens in Woodford applies at all generally in Britain, let alone in other industrial countries.

To sum up, this is the only chapter so far which has explicitly discussed the influence of social class upon family behaviour. Such contrasts as we are able to make with Woodford support those made in earlier chapters. Bethnal Greeners, who are working class almost to a man, live nearer to, and see more of, their relatives than Woodford people do; and, although to a lesser extent, the working class of

---

[1] For some evidence about the continuing importance of the bond between father and son in rural areas of the British Isles, see Williams, W. M., *The Sociology of an English Village;* Rees, A. D., *Life in a Welsh Countryside,* and Arensberg, G. M., and Kimball, S. T., *Family and Community in Ireland.*

Woodford also live nearer to their relatives and see them more often than the Woodford middle class. These findings taken together certainly suggest that social class is one of the decisive influences upon family life. If that is the first conclusion of the chapter, the second is that the working class of Woodford stands at some point on a 'kinship continuum' between Bethnal Green and the middle-class of Woodford. In family behaviour, rather more of them are like the other people of Woodford than like their fellow manual workers in Bethnal Green. The third conclusion is that movement from one class to another creates a barrier inside the family only for men, not for women. The tie between mother and daughter seems to have the strength to resist the effect of occupational change. In this chapter we have opened up the subject of class for the first time in this book. We will now proceed with it, and in the next chapter note the effect which social class has upon organizations in the borough more formal than the family.

VIII

THE ORGANIZATION OF
SOCIABILITY

ONE thing that emerges from this book so far is that relatives are seen less in the suburb. Our next question is whether people make up for this in other ways, through formal organizations, for instance, clubs, societies, churches and the like.

In Bethnal Green most people have been in the district the biggest part of their life—over half of those interviewed in the Bethnal Green general sample had been born locally, against only a tenth in the suburb. Their relatives surround them, as they do not in Woodford, and every relative provides yet more links with other people. Bethnal Greeners often work near their homes—a third work in the borough and two-thirds of the remainder elsewhere in the East End— whereas barely a quarter of Woodford people who work, do so inside their borough. The informal ties that abound in the East End—ties with relatives who are also neighbours, with neighbours who are former schoolmates or present workmates, with a whole host of people familiar in one way or another—all these make for easy, unforced sociability. Of course, there are clubs in Bethnal Green—the place is well supplied with University Settlements and youth clubs, and there are the usual British Legion branches, political organizations and the rest—but for most people these are not essential for meeting others and mixing with them. The Bethnal Greener can do enough of that without joining anything. Sociability, in such a setting, needs no organization.

The official guide to Woodford asserts that an 'outstanding feature of this Borough is its wealth of organizations and amenities devoted to the development of every aspect of social life'.[1] It is a conventional claim, but not an idle one. Certainly our impression from the interviews in both places was that clubs and like organizations played a fuller part in Woodford. Anyone who visited, as one of us did, a meeting of the Woodford Green Women's Institute, would be left in no doubt about the ability of Woodford residents—Woodford women, in this instance—to organize and sustain a flourishing organization. The hall filled with over two hundred attentive women sitting in rows of tip-up seats, the select Committee members on the flower-decked platform, the polite welcome from the Vice-President, the President delivering her announcements—this was the routine of an ordinary meeting. The President spoke about the drama group, the choir, the reading group, the Shakespeare circle, the produce guild, the handicrafts section, the icing class, before announcing the visiting speaker. After the speech—about sociology and Woodford—the important business began. Tea was served by a well-drilled corps of helpers, model hats and coconut-ice sold with immense enthusiasm from the stalls at the back of the hall. 'We're the largest branch in Essex', a bright-eyed member said—and one could well believe it.

Woodford Green, at the northern end of the borough, is outside the London postal region and, being therefore deemed 'rural', has a Women's Institute. Half a mile nearer Charing Cross is 'urban' and so has a Townswomen's Guild, also with a thriving membership. 'When we started it', said Mrs. Young, 'we organized a meeting at the Majestic Cinema. We expected about fifty people to come, but over three hundred turned up. We have meetings once a month. We always have a speaker—last year we had people like the chief Yeoman of the Tower of London, a man from Trinity

[1] *Wanstead and Woodford Official Guide* 1958–9, p. 43. The *Guide* lists as many as 142 different clubs and associations—and it is not an exhaustive list.

House on lighthouses, a lady who had just come back from Algeria, and a demonstration of ice-cream making by a man from Wall's. I go to the Guild's handicrafts class as well.'

Many of the women interviewed belonged to one of these two organizations, and often to others as well. Mrs. Robinson was a member of the Women's Institute, the Women's Gas Federation, and the Women's Section of the Conservative Party. 'I'm a committee member of the Women's Section', she said, 'We helped to run some stalls at the fête last month when Sir Winston came along.' Mrs. Barber belonged to the Townswomen's Guild, the Conservative Association and a knitting circle. About the Conservatives, she said, 'We only go to the meetings when there's a good speaker. We don't usually go to the ordinary business meetings.' As for the knitting party, 'That's every Wednesday afternoon at someone's house. We all take it in turns.'

These were two of the older women interviewed. The older men belonged to the bowls or golf club, the Conservative Club or the Rotary. Mr. Coote told us, 'I go along to the bowls club nearly every day in the summer.' Mr. Cuthbertson said, 'I go to the golf club about three times a week. I belong to the Woodford Wells Cricket and Tennis Club as well. I used to play cricket and my wife played tennis—we don't play now, but we still support the club. We always go to the cocktail party at the beginning of the season, and usually to one or two of their other functions.' Mr. Cooney belongs to the golf club, the bowls club, the Essex Bee-Keepers' Association and the Conservative Club—'I'm not strongly political. I go over there to play snooker two or three times a week.'

The younger couples with children were more likely to belong to Parent-Teacher Associations—reflecting their interest in education—or to tennis clubs and the like. Mr. and Mrs. Ashwood belong to a Parent-Teacher Association —'We're naturally interested in our children's school', Mrs. Ashwood said, 'and it's easy for us to get to the meetings and socials because it's only just round the corner. The children know the telephone number of the school and if anything went wrong they could ring us up.' Mrs. Hammond reported in her diary:

> '4 p.m. Made a telephone call to an elderly friend to see if she could sit-in for us on Thursday evening in order that we may attend a Parent-Teachers Annual General Meeting—particularly interesting to us as we have Susan in her fourth year and 11-plus imminent.'

Mr. and Mrs. Baxter are both very active in a local tennis club. So are Mr. and Mrs. Day—"We're a tennis and badminton family,' Mr. Day said. Mrs. Davis belongs 'to a badminton club and to the Young Wives' League at the church'. Mr. and Mrs. Milner belong to the Conservative Association —'but we don't go'—and Mrs. Milner attends at the League of Health and Beauty every week. Mrs. Chambers described, in her diary, her afternoon visit to a 'Keep Fit' class with a neighbour:

> '1.10. After lunch washed the dishes, cleaned downstairs, then washed and changed into my P.T. tunic. I usually wear my slacks and a jacket over the P.T. kit, as these are easier to take off when we get to the class.
> 2.30. Called for Daphne and we set off complete with two string bags containing balls. We met Enid outside the church hall where the class is held, and went in together. We always join in everything and feel better physically for the exercise. We have now reached the stage where we can do the various exercises and not feel too stiff afterwards.'

There is obviously immense variety of organization— from the Park Residents' Society to the Floral Arrangement Group, the Monkhams Singers to the Knighton Players, the Snaresbrook Ladies' Hockey Club to the Aldersbrook Tennis Club, the Archery Association to the Snaresbrook Riding School. Whether the avowed purpose is to play golf or squash, to act or sing, to advance the cause of literature or Conservatism, the United Nations or local trade—whatever the *overt* purpose, one result is that you meet other people.

What sort? In particular, what class? Table XIII compares club attendance and membership according to social class.

TABLE XIII

CLUB MEMBERSHIP AND ATTENDANCE ACCORDING TO
SOCIAL CLASS

(General sample)

	Middle Class	Working Class
Attended at least one club in the previous month ..	35%	18%
Not attended in previous month, but member of at least one club	17%	16%
Not member of any club ..	48%	66%
Total %	100%	100%
Number	580	355

Clubs and other organizations plainly attract middle-class people more than working-class. Nearly twice as many in the middle class had attended in the previous month, and over half belong to an organization, compared with a third of working-class people. This is not peculiar to Woodford. Cauter and Downham found in Derby that middle-class people were 'easily the most interested in joining clubs; not only do more of them belong to a club, but when they do join they are more likely to join more than one club'.[1] Bottomore, studying voluntary organizations in the country town of 'Squirebridge', found much the same there.[2]

There is only one kind of club which middle-class people generally do not attend—that specifically addressed to old

---

[1] Cauter, T., and Downham, J. S., *The Communication of Ideas*, p. 66.
[2] Bottomore, T., 'Social Stratification in Voluntary Organization'.

people. Only fourteen people altogether—7% of the 210 in the old age sample—belonged to 'Darby and Joan' clubs, eleven of them working-class, the other three being the wives or widows of clerks. One criticism of these clubs was that they reminded people of their age—'I can't bring myself to join one of these Darby and Joan clubs', said a retired dairy-man, 'I don't like to feel I'm that old'. An old woman re-marked, 'They get morbid at those places'. But evidently the clubs do help to meet the needs of some. Mrs. Charles, the widow of a docker, wrote this about the club she attends every week:

> 'Tuesday I go to the old peoples club. I like the club very much. Mrs. Dawson, that is the head one of the club, plays the piano and they all sing. They play cards, some sit and chat, men play darts and dominoes and ludo. About 2.30 we have a cup of tea and home-made cake, very nice. Then about three o'clock Mrs. Dawson gives out some notices. We are going to Palladium on May 29th. After that she plays piano until four o'clock. We pay twopence membership fee and twopence a cup of tea and cake, raffles one penny each.'

We have so far ignored church attendance, though we have included clubs linked to churches. But churchgoing, the subject of Table XIV, shows a similar class difference. The connexion between social class and church attendance has also been observed in other inquiries. Linking a national survey by the B.B.C. with that of Cauter and Downham in Derby, a recent book summed up: 'Frequent church-going becomes markedly less common with decline in the social scale.'[1]

Even among the middle class in Woodford regular weekly church-going is the practice of only a minority. But well over half the middle-class people said they attended some-times, quite enough to make the local churches busy places.

[1] Carr-Saunders, A. M., Jones, D. C., and Moser, C. A., *Social Conditions in England and Wales*, p. 261.

TABLE XIV

CHURCH ATTENDANCE ACCORDING TO SOCIAL CLASS

(General sample)

	Middle Class	*Working Class*
Attended within previous month	34%	17%
Not attended within previous month but go to church ..	26%	26%
Never go to church	40%	57%
Total %	100%	100%
Number	580	355

As one woman said, 'Lots of people go to church in Woodford. On a Sunday morning it's a job to get in at St. Mary's.'[1] Children sometimes make it difficult to attend. Mrs. Chambers, married to a manager and with three children, said, 'We don't get to church every Sunday, but we try to get there most Sundays, morning or evening. We couldn't go when the children were younger, but now they're a bit bigger, the whole family tries to go every week.' Mrs. Davis said, 'My son goes to Sunday School, and I usually take him at Easter and Christmas and special occasions like that. About half a dozen times a year my friend over the road and I arrange to look after the other's children, so as to allow us to go to Communion with our husbands.' Mrs. Day reported in her diary for Sunday:

'5 p.m. Had tea and then all changed for church. After the

---

[1] Woodford is apparently, however, not very different from the country as a whole. In the general sample, 15 % of people had attended church in the previous week. The proportion attending, 'once a week or more', was found by Gorer in a national study to be 15 % (Gorer, G., *Exploring English Character*, p. 241). In Derby, it was 13 % (Cauter, T., and Downham, J. S., op. cit., p. 52). The Gallup Poll, in February 1957, found that 14% had been to church on the previous Sunday.

service, instead of the Vicar's sermon we had a talk from a Missionary Doctor on leave from Nigeria. We listened with interest, but the kiddies found it a little drawn-out, especially as it was rather cold in church'.

Among those without young children, the church is more often an absorbing interest. Miss Allan is a retired school-teacher who lives alone and has no relatives in Woodford. She is a regular attender at the church round the corner from where she lives, is in charge of the choir at the church, runs a small ladies' choir that meets at her home, is the Registrar of the Sunday School and the leader of the ladies' working party. Altogether, as she put it herself, 'practically every evening' is spent on activities connected with the church. Mrs. Panton, the wife of a shop assistant, said, 'I go to a Church Fellowship every Thursday afternoon and I'm on the Committee and I help them with sales of work and so on. Once I gave a talk to them and I'm now on the rota. All the family goes to church on Sunday morning. My husband's in the choir and in the afternoon I go to play the piano at the Sunday School. I love that.' The previous Sunday she had not done this because her husband was singing at the Congregational Church and she had to play for him on the piano; 'My elder daughter took my place at Sunday School'. Her husband is a sidesman at church. Mr. Cunningham, a retired auditor, is treasurer for a charitable fund run by the church he attends. 'The accounts take up quite a lot of my time,' he said.

These three were all office-holders and they were all middle-class. Even where manual workers belonged to clubs they were very seldom office-holders—Presidents, Chairmen, Secretaries, Treasurers and so on. This is not a question we explored systematically in Woodford—we did not ask everyone if he or she held office in an organization. But our impression there would certainly be consistent with what is known of other areas—both in Derby and in 'Squirebridge', the county town studied by Bottomore, leadership in churches, clubs and other organizations is undoubtedly the preserve of the middle and upper classes.[1] In this, Woodford, it seems, is like the country generally.

One reason may simply be that middle-class people have more of the right experience—Mr. Cunningham, for instance, as a retired auditor, was an obvious candidate as Treasurer for his church; a managing director who can run a business can obviously run a tennis club; a clerk is likely to be thought more competent at taking the minutes of a meeting than a carpenter. Unless they are very active members of a trade union, working-class people do not ordinarily obtain as much administrative experience in the course of their working lives as middle-class people do. This is obvious enough.

We also asked about attendance at public houses, where, remembering the pub's popularity in Bethnal Green, we expected a difference. It turned out otherwise—in the suburb, working-class people go even to pubs less frequently than their middle-class neighbours, as Table XV shows.

One reason may be that Woodford's manual workers—particularly those buying their own houses—have less money, less time and less inclination to go to pubs than those in the East End. Another explanation may be the character of Woodford's pubs. They are not small cosy bars of the Bethnal Green type, filled with the cheerful jangle of a honky-tonk piano or a twanging juke-box. They are, quite often, much larger places, with carpeted lounges furnished in pseudo-Jacobean style, where the landlords wear crested blazers and call their customers 'old boy', and where the drinks are much more often pink gins or whiskies and soda than pints of mild and bitter. The public bars are very much pushed off at the side. Bricklayers, dockers and motor fitters might easily feel ill-at-ease in such surroundings.

Working class excluded

We have established the fact that working-class people in

---

[1] Cauter, T., and Downham, J. S., op. cit., p. 73. Bottomore, T., op. cit., p. 368 and p. 381.

TABLE XV

ATTENDANCE AT PUBLIC HOUSE[1] ACCORDING TO SOCIAL CLASS

(General sample)

	Middle Class	Working Class
Attended within previous month	47%	35%
Not attended within previous month but sometimes go	21%	22%
Do not go	32%	43%
Total %	100%	100%
Number	580	355

Woodford seldom belong to clubs or attend church. Why is it? Some people suggested that expense was the barrier.'How could I afford nineteen guineas to join the golf club even if I wanted to', a crane driver put it. 'You've got to have money in your pocket to belong to a club or anything like that', said a labourer's wife. Others explained that they could not spare the time. 'By the time I come home', said a railway worker, 'there's only time to have something to eat and take it easy by the TV.' 'I don't get time for anything like that', an electrician said. A docker explained that he was too exhausted by his heavy manual job: 'I don't know about other people, I'm too tired for all that. When I come home I've had it. It's all taken out of me.'

But these, we believe, are not the only explanations. Another may be, as we said earlier, that the working class do not feel welcome in many of Woodford's clubs and societies.

[1] Or 'hotel bar'. Herein lies one of the differences from the East End. In pilot interviews, some middle-class people insisted that they had not been into a public house, but into an 'hotel bar'. We changed the question to read 'When did you last go into a public house or hotel bar?'

Most people feel more comfortable with members of what they think of as their own social class. Middle-class people in particular, seeking to create a kind of 'community' for themselves through organizations, want fellows with whom they feel at ease. A businessman remarked about a club he and his wife had visited, but only once, 'You get all sorts there, and in this wicked world all sorts don't mix'. Sometimes consciously, sometimes not, the middle class who predominate keep others out. In some districts, manual workers counter this by creating Working Men's Clubs and other one-class organizations of their own, but they do not do this to any extent in Woodford.

Most organizations in the suburb are not explicitly selective in their membership, though there are exceptions. The Rotary Club, for instance, is specifically reserved for people in professional and executive positions, and the Chamber of Commerce ('It should really be called the Chamber of Trade, but commerce has a snob value') is open only to local traders.

Other clubs effectively control membership with high fees or by more subtle means. 'Supposing a plasterer or someone like that applied to join', one club member told us, 'We want something a little bit higher social standard than that.' 'When a new chap wants to join', he added, 'he has to give members as references. We say to them, "This chap wants to join. What do you know about him?" ' Another informant said of a sports club:

'We welcome anybody who likes a good game. We wouldn't turn a man down for class prejudice, you understand. But we can't let our status down either. He must be able to mix, a good fellow socially. A new member has to be proposed and seconded and no member would introduce a friend he didn't think acceptable.' He added that there were other clubs that his club wouldn't play against: 'They play well, but socially they're not the same. We gave one of them a game not so long ago—it stood out a mile they were of a different standing. I don't mean to be snobbish, but there it is.'

Some clubs would have liked working-class members, but

found that if they came they seldom stayed. One wife, active in a cultural society, said, 'Anybody is welcome to join. But our members are mostly middle class, products of private schools, educated people.' Another remarked, 'The idea was to get a cross-section of members. But the debates kept away the less intelligent. Now we are all middle class—we are all friends actually.' The wife of a bank manager said about the club she belonged to, 'The intellectual ones increased and the unintellectual ones stopped coming. Now we've all got similar sorts of interests.' In Woodford, as in 'Squire-bridge', 'Consciously or unconsciously some of the organizations discourage or squeeze out individuals with lower occupational status'.[1]

To sum up, Woodford is certainly rich in social organizations. In the suburb, the middle class can—and do—enjoy the varied social life that is offered by the churches, the golf and tennis clubs, the dramatic societies and choirs. All these help them to meet others and make up for their newness and the absence of relatives. Woodford's working class do not belong so often. Institutional sociability has little to offer them. They go some way towards making up for this by having more to do with their wider families. Do they also make up for it by informal contacts with friends and neighbours? This question is taken up in the next chapter.

[1] Bottomore, T., op. cit., p. 368.

IX

THE PATTERN OF FRIENDSHIP

THE previous chapter was about clubs, churches and other organizations. This one is about friends. The function of the one is to introduce the other. Some of the people first met at church, at the tennis club or the drama society and became friends later. 'We didn't know many people', said Mr. Milner, 'until my wife got going with the Health and Beauty lark. We've met quite a lot of people through that.' Likewise Mr. and Mrs. Day.

'We have a lot of friends round here. We know a lot of people—people connected with the church, and with the badminton and tennis. Not only the church, where we go every week and see the same people, but also the organizations connected with it.'

It can work the other way round too—the new face at the whist drive may be the old face of a next-door neighbour. Or a person may invite a friend to a meeting. Mrs. Prior, for instance, always calls for a friend to go with her to the dressmaking class. Other people made no sharp distinction between membership and friendship.

'There are about fifty people I know from the church', Miss Quibell said, 'I see lots of them regularly and often stop for a chat. Then there are about twenty more I've got to know through the National Savings movement. A lot of these people are old friends and neighbours as well.'

'I've got dozens of friends here', said Mrs. Baxter, who was born in the district, 'Some I've known nearly all my life, others I've met through tennis and squash, others are the friends of friends I've made through tennis and squash.'

The active club members have friends in more often—of the 177 people in the general sample who had attended a club in the previous week, 83% had been visited by a non-relative during the same period, against 69% of the 548 who never go to a club. But clubs and other organizations by no means account for all the friendships in Woodford—after all, over two-thirds even of those who do not belong had some friends in.

Indeed, a remarkably high proportion of all people had friends or neighbours into their homes. Altogether 39% of the 939 people in the general sample had had a 'friend or neighbour' in during the previous twenty-four hours, and a further 34% earlier in the previous week. In other words, nearly three-quarters (73%) had a visitor at some time during the week. Relatives, as earlier chapters have shown, played a small part—24% had been visited in the home by a relative in the previous twenty-four hours, 33% at some other time in the previous week, making only 57% altogether.

Friends are local

Most of the visitors, it turns out, were living in Woodford. There were two exceptions to this. Firstly, some people entertained business or professional colleagues whose homes were in a different district. 'We had Jack's boss and his wife to dinner last Tuesday', said the wife of a sales manager, 'They live out at Theydon Bois.' 'I quite often bring a business colleague back here for a drink or a meal', said a manager just elevated to his firm's board of directors. Senior executives apart, most people did not go in for 'business entertaining' of this kind.

Secondly, people often had a few friends living at a distance —former neighbours or school friends or colleagues—whom they kept up with. Mrs. Martin said, 'My friend at Birmingham—well it's Selly Oak, really, where they live—I've known her all my life. Sometimes we hire a car and drive up to see them at the week-end. Sometimes they come down here. They've got their own car.' Mrs. Chambers reported in her diary:

'Had a very enjoyable telephone conversation with a friend, now living in Kent. We arranged to meet in Town one day next week, and also for them to visit us as soon as they have "fixed up the rear lights on the car". My husband and I are fond of them both and missed them a lot when they moved to Kent, due entirely to business reasons.'

But, like other people, both Mrs. Martin and Mrs. Chambers, though they kept in touch with these friends in other districts, naturally saw more of those living closer. In the main, the friends who figured most in people's daily lives not only lived in Woodford; they lived in the immediate neighbourhood, often in the same or next road.

'I've got a lot of friends', said Mrs. Long, 'most of them in Corncroft Crescent. There's Mary at number four, Eileen at sixteen, another friend at twenty-four, another at twenty-nine and another at twenty-one. They're all friends I've made since we moved here.' 'I've got a very good friend over the road whom I see almost every day', said Mrs. Davis, 'If we want to borrow anything or have a natter we go and call on each other. I've got another friend up the road, another one round the corner, another one round in Walton Drive. I've got quite a lot of very good friends round here.' 'We've got quite a little circle of friends in the vicinity', said Mr. Prior, 'We have quite a lot of parties and the people are mostly from around here.' 'We all get on very well in this road', said Mrs. Sturgis, 'Every morning someone takes it in turn to have the others in for coffee.' 'The lady at number eight is a very good friend', said Mrs. Clark, 'I've got a lot of other friends round here—they're all very sociable in this part.' An excerpt from her diary illustrates what she meant:

'10.30. Was just finishing off the washing when my friend Phyllis arrived. She lives a few doors away, and we have a great deal in common and enjoy each other's company. This morning she brought in two of her special cakes to sample. She had had company at the week-end—some of her friends whom she described as "nouveaux riches"—and had made some cakes for their benefit. While I finished the washing and made some coffee, we discussed the party we had both been to on Saturday, and also the possibility of going to an Auction together.

11.45. Phyllis was just about to go when my friend Peggy called. She lives across the road and has three children much the same ages as my own. She had promised to come over this afternoon, but her elder son was not well, so she came over to invite me to go over there instead for half an hour. She and Phyllis started a discussion about refrigerators.'

Not all belong to a group of local friends, as do those quoted so far, but most people have at least *one* friend living nearby—someone to whom they feel they can turn. This applies particularly to the wives, who need companionship and aid while their husbands are at work during the day. Most distinguish between their 'friend' or 'friends' and other people living nearby. 'We're friendly with everybody', said Mrs. Holmes, 'but not to the extent of going into each other's houses—except for my friend down the road.' Mrs. Bates had two special friends, but made the same point: 'Apart from my two friends along the road, I don't go into people's houses, but I do stop and have a chatter with some of them. We all say "Good morning" and "Good afternoon" as we go up and down the road, and sometimes we just stop and talk about the weather or their children or how they are. They're all very nice people, though we don't know them intimately.'

The common pattern, it seems, is to belong to a small, intimate network of 'friends', mostly coming from the surrounding twenty or thirty houses, though some people, particularly in professional or managerial jobs, also have friends living farther afield. The size of this local network varies—sometimes it is just a pair, sometimes three or four, sometimes ten or twelve, sometimes an even larger group. This system, largely organized by the women, is the analogue to the 'extended family' of the East End. Outside are the other local residents—the 'neighbours', as they are often called, though some people, as in the country generally, apply this term only to those in immediately adjacent houses.[1] With these, people are 'friendly', though they are not 'friends'. Some informants stressed the importance of maintaining social distance—'We don't get familiar or over-friendly with the neighbours', Mrs. Brady said. And some, who had come from the East End, felt that Woodford was less welcoming to strangers, less friendly and easy-going, than the boroughs they had left. 'Woodford is a very cold affair compared with Bethnal Green', Mrs. Clarkson said, 'The people aren't unpleasant but they aren't neighbours or friends in the close sense.' It was our impression, too, from interviewing in both places, that though people in the East End might act as host to fewer personal friends outside the family, social relationships were more closely knit and loyalties stronger there.

But most people in Woodford seem to like their fellow-residents, a majority of the general sample saying that the people around them are 'easy to get on with'. Nearly two-thirds (64%) held this opinion, against a quarter who said they 'didn't notice them much', and less than a tenth who thought them 'inclined to be standoffish'. 'They're very friendly round this district', said Mrs. Sankey. 'There's a very friendly spirit', Mrs. Noble remarked, 'I think it's a wonderful community in this part.' This in contradiction to a fashionable stereotype of the suburb—anxious, footloose migrants, somehow keeping themselves to themselves and yet up with the Jones's. The people of Woodford felt they belonged to a friendly, helpful community almost as unanimously as the people of Bethnal Green.

Making friends

We were more struck by the contrast with the municipal housing estate we had previously compared with Bethnal Green. There, at Greenleigh, people both thought the place unfriendly and seldom had others into their home, even after they had been there five or six years. In Woodford it is plainly

---

[1] See Gorer, G., *Exploring English Character*, p. 52.

different. 'I've been in Woodford four years', said Mrs. Humphreys, 'And I've made lots of friends.'

The kind of people who move into the suburb, mostly into houses of their own, seem to have no difficulty in getting to know each other and make friends. They are something like the transients at Park Forest, the privately-developed 'new town' near Chicago for middle-class executives described by Whyte in *The Organization Man*.[1] In both Park Forest and Woodford, to talk, as people often do, about the problem of 'roots' is to miss the point. It is true that one woman who had lived in Woodford for six years said, 'I think the difficulty is all this moving around. If we'd lived in one place longer, we'd have put down more roots.' What was striking about this statement was that it was unique—nobody else said anything remotely similar. Most people, particularly the younger couples, have no such problem. Like the Park Foresters, they seem to have the capacity to put down roots quickly wherever they live. Some even think it desirable to move from time to time to make a new set of friends—'If you stay in one place a long time', one wife said, 'you tend to get into a rut. It's better to uproot yourself and make new friends.'

Things are certainly made easy for the right kind of new-comer. 'The day I moved into this house', Mrs. Jackson said, 'the lady opposite—whom I'd never seen before in my life—told the milkman to leave a pint of milk and call back again at dinner-time to see what we wanted.' 'My wife', explained Mr. Matthews, 'is the sort of person who endeavours to entertain new people whenever they arrive. If anyone new comes to live on this estate, they're invited to one of her coffee even-ings.' Mrs. King was taking her dog for a walk soon after she had arrived when another young woman living in the same road went up to her and asked, 'Were you in the Wrens?' 'She didn't know I had been', Mrs. King told us, 'She'd never met me before, but she said she just guessed I'd been in the Wrens like her.' Now they are close friends.

[1] Whyte, W. H., *The Organization Man*, Chapter 22.

Others too make friends through the daily walk with their dog. Miss Spark explained, 'Having a little dog is a great help in getting to know people. People stop and talk to you about the dog and then you get talking about other things.' But children are the biggest aid. 'You get to know people through your children', said Mrs. Ross, 'You walk along and it's "Hullo, Alan", "Hullo, Susan. This is the little girl we play with". Her mother is with her, so we stop and talk.' Mrs. Holmes explained, 'I met my friend three doors down because her little girl Ann started school when mine did. Now Ann spends nearly as much time here as in her own home.' 'All the people round here are much the same age', said Mrs. Swift, 'And they've all got young children, so they've got much the same interests.' Others had not been so fortunate. 'When we first came there was mostly an older generation on the estate', said Mr. Burgess, 'We found it difficult to make friends of our own age with children.' 'When a FOR SALE board goes up', said another wife, who was in a road with many older people, 'we hope it means a young couple with children will be moving in.'

The young couples certainly provide a good deal of practical help to each other. 'My friend along the road has got two children herself', Mrs. Baxter told us, 'I see her every day because we do a duty rota together, fetching the children to and from school. We take it in turns.' 'When my husband was ill this summer', Mrs. Day said, 'Mrs. Faulkner over the road had my children in to tea quite a lot.' They help in other ways as well. 'Yesterday morning I trotted over to Edna', said Mrs. Davis, 'I said, "I'm going up the High Street. Does anybody want any bread?" We found three or four wanted it, so I went up and got it for them with the rest of my shopping. We always get bread for the others if we go to the shops.' Mrs. Long and her friends 'take it in turns to have the others in to tea. We have a cup of tea and talk for an hour or two. It's very good because it gives everyone a break with the kiddies.' Friends nearby also helped people when they were ill in bed. 'There's a friend down the road who I see several times a week', said Mrs. Martin, 'She helped out.' 'I've got a very good friend', Mrs. Ashwood told us, 'She came in every day.'

We showed in Chapter III that young couples in the suburb see little of relatives, and do not depend to any great extent on the extended family for regular help or companionship. We can now see whom they do turn to. They create, with people of their own age, a group—sometimes small, sometimes large—with functions somewhat similar to those of the East End extended family.

It is organized, as the extended family is, by the women, the husbands being drawn into it in a similar sort of way. Its basis is not the kinship tie between mother and daughter, but the bond of common interest between wives with young children. The women often treat each other almost as if they were related. 'We're more like sisters than friends', Mrs. Kendrick said of the woman living opposite her. The children grow up to call their mother's friends 'Auntie'—'Only to-day', Mrs. Hammond said, 'I had to go to the West End and my little boy went over to stay with Auntie Dorothy. That's what the children call my friend over the road.'

Friendship and age

In the main, the pattern we have been describing is that of the younger couples with children. Older people, particularly over 70, have less friends, as Table XVI shows.

Some of the older residents of Woodford have lost their former friends—they have died, gone to join their own children elsewhere, or retired to Westcliff, Bournemouth or Torquay. 'On the whole we see less of friends now', said Mrs. Lambert, 'The reason is very much because they've moved away.' 'I've only one friend left in Woodford', said Mrs. Robertson, who is 70, 'The others have moved all over the place—Pembroke, Cornwall, Norfolk, Amersham and Newmarket.' As they grow older other people withdraw from society. Mr. Stockman, who is 76, said, 'We stay in most of the time now and just enjoy each other's company. We don't entertain much any more.'

Table XVI

Friends Visiting, according to Age

(General sample)

	20–39	40–49	50–59	60–69	70 and over
People visited by friend or neighbour in previous week	80%	76%	74%	69%	53%
Total number ..	319	212	213	105	70

Others have themselves moved into the district fairly recently—a fifth of all those over 60 had come in the past ten years, mostly to join children—and find it more difficult to make friends at that age. Kinship increases in importance with advancing age, friendship declines. Yet the old people were not usually entirely dependent on family for assistance and companionship—we gathered plenty of examples of help given to old people by friends and neighbours.

'We're all very neighbourly here. We always do a bit of shopping for each other—the woman next door asks if I want anything when she's going out, and I do the same for her. Last week I was in their house every day—they were away on holiday and I went in to water their plants for them.'

'A neighbour came in to mend our fuse on Saturday night', a widow told us, 'He's very good that way. If there's any digging in the garden, the neighbours won't let us do it: the men come in and do it. Last week Mr. Smithson along the road came and creosoted our fence for us.'

'Next door but one has pussy when we go on holiday. Last year she broke her arm and I used to go in and help her. One day I said, "I can't possibly leave pussy with you this year, Miss Kenyon, you won't be able to manage with your arm in plaster". She said, "Nonsense, of course I'll have pussy as usual. She'll be company for me." Wasn't that nice of her?'

Age is not the only thing that affects social relationships in the suburb. Where your house is can make a difference. (We do not mean which *district* of Woodford it is in; we come to that in the next chapter.) A main road, for example, may not be as friendly as a side road. Mrs. Phillips, who had recently moved, explained, 'We never got neighbourly where we lived before on the main road. They're exactly the same type of people in this road as they were there, but here you can get to know them, on a main road you can't.' Mrs. Reynolds had a different complaint: 'Living at the end of the road here, we don't see much of the neighbours. My back door looks on to the allotments—you could stand there all day and not see anyone at all.' This is not a subject we studied systematically, but there is enough evidence from other inquiries to show that location can have some influence on relationships with fellow-residents.[1]

Temperament is of even greater importance. 'It's up to you whether people are friendly or not', said Mrs. Franklin, 'When I first came here I didn't make many friends. Then I got over the shock of parting from my relations and found it wasn't so bad here.' 'I find people are very much as you treat them', Mrs. Browning said. 'If you approach people pleasantly and in a co-operative kind of way, then they'll be the same to you. It's up to the individual.' It seems that if you are new to a suburb like Woodford, it is no good being shy. In a long-established community like Bethnal Green it may not matter much, you will have an active social life anyway. Not in Woodford. As one wife said, 'We're too independent. I know that. You've got to be prepared to go out and *make* friends.' Those who find this difficult, or who feel unable to join in easily with their fellows, may suffer. 'Unless you're in the swing, like being an active Conservative', said the wife of a commercial traveller, 'suburbia is *hell*.'

---

[1] Whyte, W. H., op. cit., pp. 336–49, and Festinger, L., Schacter, S., and Back, K., *Social Pressures in Informal Groups*. The influence of layout and location are also discussed in the forthcoming survey of Dagenham by Peter Willmott.

Friendship and social class

Finally, there is the influence of social class. The picture we have drawn—of young couples in owner-occupied houses striking up quick friendships with their fellows—is predominantly a middle-class one. Working-class people do not have friends in so often, as Table XVII indicates.

TABLE XVII

FRIENDS VISITING, ACCORDING TO SOCIAL CLASS

(General sample)

Last visit from friend or neighbour was:	Middle Class	Working Class
In previous 24 hours	42%	34%
Earlier in previous week	36%	33%
Not in previous week	22%	33%
Total %	100%	100%
Number	580	355

As with clubs and church, manual workers have less of a social life outside the family. Again, this may be partly just because they have more to do with relatives—'I'm not one to make friends', a carpenter's wife said, 'I think it's because I see so much of the family.'

But, quite apart from this, some working-class people expressed objections to allowing non-relatives into the home. 'I never have neighbours in', said one woman, 'The only people who come in here are my mother and my sister-in-law.' 'We don't believe in going in and out of other people's houses', another wife told us. An older woman said proudly, 'I've never had strangers in here since the day I moved in.' And another, 'I don't hold with that sort of thing.' Clearly, working-class people in Woodford are in yet another way different from their middle-class neighbours.

On the whole there is no doubt at all that most people regard Woodford as a friendly place, and that young middle-class residents at any rate usually have plenty of 'friends' nearby as well. It is friendly in a different way from the East End, relying less on long-standing connexions between one family and another, and more on a kind of effort to be sociable. But the conclusion is that, however it is done, many people in Woodford have found in a circle of friends some at least of the society and some of the warmth which in Bethnal Green is provided by the extended family.

X

THE TENSIONS OF SOCIAL CLASS

I F we are right in what we have said in this book so far, social class is the key to understanding many of the differences in the suburb. Working-class people behave differently from middle-class in many ways. But we have said little about how people in Woodford themselves see the social classes to which they belong.

The division we have used throughout—into 'middle class' and 'working class'—is obviously an over-simplified one. Not everybody in Woodford draws the lines between the classes exactly as we have drawn them. Nor is either class as much of a unity as we may have seemed to suggest. Some people in the middle class, to begin with, were certainly conscious of divisions within it. 'Some of the parents at the school seem to put it on a bit', said Mr. Prior, a bank manager whose children go to a local preparatory school, 'You do get a bit of the old blue-blooded attitude among them.' 'Some of the people we meet seem to be a little bit snooty', said Mrs. Liversidge, an underwriter's wife. And a surveyor gave an account which showed that he himself was not entirely free from a sense of social superiority.

'We have a very dear friend at Woodford Green who's a practising barrister. It never struck us that people might like to know them just because he was a barrister, but when the wife's needlework group had a meeting there, some of the wives were very pleased just because he was a barrister. Some of them were surprised and a bit annoyed at my wife because she just said "Hullo, Joan" to the barrister's wife.'

Such claims for superior status as are made in the suburb

are on one of two grounds. The first is what one wife called 'breeding', the 'old blue-blooded attitude' encountered by Mr. Prior, or its variation—'knowing the right people' or 'being in with the Churchill mob', as another man put it. The second is simply wealth, or at least owning the visible badges of wealth—the £8,000 house, the Rover 100, the extra-large refrigerator. 'There's all this emphasis on material possessions', complained Mrs. Davis, 'People seem to think that if they've got something you haven't got they're better than you are. And they're not really what I would call well-educated people. They're people who've got the money but not the educational background to go with it.' One man saw it from the other side:

> 'People are inclined to be rather envious. They see my big car and my caravan and I suppose it gets under their skins a bit. My children come back and say other children have been saying, "Your father must have pots of money".'

How much of this competitiveness for material goods was there among middle-class people? Informants disagreed about how general it was and how much it mattered. 'I think there is some of that sort of thing', said Mr. Green, 'People say "Mrs. So-and-so's got that and I'll get one too".' Others could cite specific examples.

> 'As soon as next door knew we'd got a washing machine', said a husband, 'they got one too. Then a few months later we got a fridge, so they got a fridge as well. I thought all this stuff about keeping up with the Jones's was just talk until I saw it happening right next door.'

One housewife's neighbour also followed her in buying a fridge.

> 'It seems to worry her if we have anything new. When she got a fridge she made a great fuss of showing that she could make ice-bricks too. She stood at the door and said, "I'm very worried the children will catch their fingers in the fridge door", just to show she'd got one.'

Cars are favourite objects of rivalry:

'During the course of conversation a neighbour told me they were getting a new car. Then she mentioned someone else in the road who's just got a new car, and she said, "That'll be a knock in the eye for *them*".'

'Two of our friends in this crescent had Morris Minors like me. I started it by changing and buying a new Ford Consul. The other two followed very shortly, and they've gone one better than me. One's got a Zephyr, the other's got an A95.'

'My wife is always getting on to me. She says, "I see the so-and-so's have got a car. Why don't *you* get a car?"'

There was also a good deal of anxiety about education. Middle-class husbands and wives cared about it for the child's own sake—'we must do all we can to see he makes the very best of his abilities', as one wife said—and for the family's. Some of the better-off parents tried to solve the problem by sending their children to private schools—Woodford boasts its own 'public school' (Bancrofts) and as many as eighteen other private schools. The lower-paid white-collar workers— bank clerks, insurance agents, teachers—could not afford to do this, and were understandably anxious that their children should do well in the state educational system, particularly in the 11-plus tests selecting children for the grammar schools that lead on to the professions and to university. Mrs. Clark, for instance, who already has a daughter at a local grammar school said, 'We don't know how the two boys will do in the eleven-plus when their turn comes, but we're *hoping*. Like most of the parents in this district, we do take an interest in our children. We encourage them all we can. You can see how important it is for them to pass.'

'Naturally enough,' said Mr. Hammond, 'parents worry about it. My wife and I have been giving her exam test papers to do, just a few to keep her up to it and she's come up from twenty-ninth to twelfth in her class in the last year. But you can't be sure, can you? All parents out here are suburbanites. To hear them talk they've *all* got children who have moved up in the class. I'm afraid Essex is a very competitive county.'

Working-class divisions

It was not only middle-class parents who worried about their children's education. Some in the working class were just as anxious that their children should do well in the 11-plus, while others, like Mr. White, a docker, 'never paid much attention to their schooling'. 'As long as they get good jobs when they leave', he said, 'that's all that matters.'

Among manual workers, too, there were some complaints about rivalry over possessions. A labourer's wife said, 'Whatever the others have got, the people next door want as well. We get a new Hoover, so she's got to have one. Another neighbour's got a new studio couch, so she's got one—and she's still paying for it.' The wife of an electrician told us, 'The lady next door likes to think she's got something better than us. If we have something done, she wants it done. We had our ceiling done—so she rushes round to the Council right away to get hers done.'

Then there were manual workers or their wives who clearly thought their own status higher than that of their fellows. 'Some of them seem to be very slummy on this estate', said a Council tenant, the wife of a bricklayer. 'Some of the people in this road are a bit rough', said another woman, married to a fitter. People like this seemed to have in mind a distinction similar to that between the 'rough' and the 'respectable' noted by other researchers in studies of working-class areas.[1]

Many manual workers have so improved their standard of life that it is increasingly 'middle class'. To them class depends not so much upon occupation or education as on income, not so much on the world of production as that of consumption. It is therefore not surprising that many of them did not consider themselves 'working-class' at all. We asked what class people thought they belonged to, and found that nearly half (48%) of the 355 manual workers in the general

[1] See Kuper, L., *Living in Towns;* Mogey, J. M., *Family and Neighbourhood;* and *Neighbourhood and Community.*

sample considered themselves middle class—3% said upper middle, 35% middle and 10% lower middle.

This is not simply a difference between skilled and unskilled manual workers—the former being more 'middle class' than the latter. Of course, by and large, the skilled workers are better paid and, therefore, one would think, more able to afford to buy a house, a car and other consumption goods. But 'middle-class' identification is hardly less frequent among the unskilled and semi-skilled than the skilled. Of the 257 skilled manual workers in the general sample, 49% said they were 'upper middle', 'middle', or 'lower middle'; of the 98 semi-skilled or unskilled 43%.

Woodford is not unique in having manual workers who put themselves into the 'middle class', only in the proportion doing so, which is higher than in other places, namely Dagenham, Greenwich and Hertford,[1] where people have been asked about it. The rule suggested by these four places is that the more the middle class predominates in a district, the more working-class people identify themselves with it, and, incidentally, the more often they vote Conservative. 'Middle-class' manual workers tend to be as much Conservative as 'working-class' manual workers are Labour.

Who are these manual workers who describe themselves as middle class? They are, to begin with, more often people who have some of the possessions that go with a middle-class style of life. Table XVIII shows this. These self-styled 'middle class' can also be distinguished from 'working class' in other important ways, as Table XIX indicates.

[1] See Martin, F. M., 'Some Subjective Aspects of Social Stratification', in *Social Mobility in Britain*, ed. D. V. Glass. 23% of Greenwich and 31% of Hertford manual workers considered themselves middle class; the proportions are calculated from Table 4 on p. 56 of the above book. The figure for Dagenham, obtained from the survey made by Peter Willmott but not yet published, is 13%. These figures are not quite comparable with those we have quoted for Woodford. In the other districts people were simply asked 'Which class do you belong to?', whereas in Woodford we began with that question and then offered people a list to choose from—Upper, Upper Middle, Middle, Lower Middle, Working, Can't Say. The proportion of Woodford manual workers assessing themselves as middle class rose from 34% judged only according to the first question, to 48% when judged according to the second.

TABLE XVIII

OWNERSHIP ACCORDING TO SELF-ASCRIBED CLASS

(Manual workers only—general sample)

	'Middle Class'	'Working Class'
Living in owner-occupied house	56%	36%
Where household has car ..	39%	20%
Where household has telephone	38%	20%
Total number	170	185

TABLE XIX

ATTENDANCE AT CHURCH AND CLUB, ACCORDING TO SELF-ASCRIBED CLASS

(Manual workers only—general sample)

	'Middle Class'	'Working Class'
Attending Church ..	52%	36%
Belonging to Clubs ..	42%	27%
Total number	170	185

In church and club membership, the manual workers who say they are 'middle class' behave more like middle-class people. They also seem to be rather like them in family relationships. For example, only 22% of the 170 'middle-class' manual workers had been visited by a relative in the previous day, but 32% of the 185 others had.

Manual workers are in this and other ways divided amongst themselves, and so, we saw earlier, are the non-manual. Neither of the classes is homogeneous. But while divided among themselves they might still be united against each other. Their relations to each other is the subject to which we now turn.

Relations between classes

Most middle-class people recognized that the status of the manual workers is changing. Mr. Martin said, 'Woodford's mostly middle class. As a matter of fact the country's getting middle class altogether. The poor have almost vanished.' 'The middle class has spread out', said Mr. Davis, 'It has moved down to include some who used to be lower class, and some of the upper class has merged in with it too.' Others were less sanguine about accepting the trend. They acknowledged but did not welcome the fact that manual wages had risen. 'It seems to me', said one wife, 'it's the so-called lower classes who're better off than anybody else these days.' 'Poor people, so-called, are earning more than the middle class today', said a clerk. 'It's the people like me,' complained the widow of a Civil Servant, living on a fixed pension, 'who are the sufferers these days. The people who work with their hands—what would you call them, the working class, I suppose—seem to be getting the best of it now.'

Higher wages do not necessarily make middle-class people feel that the workers are *socially* higher than they used to be; indeed some of them speak as though the workers were more to be looked down on than ever since they attained prosperity. Two sticks were used. The first was the time-honoured one about the British workman, that he did not work. 'The working class is wrongly named', said a company director, 'because they don't work at all, judging by what happens in our firm.' 'They don't seem to want to try these days', agreed a factory manager. 'The workers don't pull their weight', a wife said, 'I'm going by all those men I see leaning on their shovels. If they can get out of working they will.'

The other complaint, commoner and more deeply felt, was that the working class do not know how to spend all their extra money—that they have got a middle-class income without the ingrained middle-class sense of how to spend it. The white-collar people who argue like this are not prepared to recognize the distinction themselves between 'middle-class' and 'working-class' manual workers. All are equally open to criticism. 'The working class is better off', said one woman, 'which is a good thing *if* they know how to use their money. Which they don't, I'm sorry to say.' A Civil Servant's wife agreed:

> 'The people who've made the most money since the war are the lower classes, but they don't seem to know how to spend it wisely. The ordinary sort of person—I suppose you'd call them middle class—the sort of people who put their family first, they haven't done too well. I've often noticed that the people who've got the money these days don't spend it on their families but on the dogs and such things.'

> 'I think the richest class today', said a works manager, 'is the working class, and they don't know how to spend their money. They waste money on fridges, washing machines, TVs and cars. It's the old tale—the person born to money knows how to use it, the person new to getting it doesn't.'

The bitterest attacks seemed to come from people who were close to the boundary between working and middle class, whose own job had dropped in status or financial reward, or whose own future was insecure. The commercial traveller whose trade—women's hats—was declining. The clerk who said, 'I like to think I'm in the middle class but I suppose I'm in the working class. I know the fitters at our place take home more than I do. But look what they spend it on.' The teacher who said, 'I suppose before the war I'd be middle class. Teachers had a high social standing then, but now professional people are the lowest. At least that's in money. Actually, we're a pretty high class.'

If the distinctions are to be maintained, then obviously it will not do for the critics to mix too intimately with the working class. The middle class are generally on good terms with the neighbours, as we have seen, and make friends easily. But this only holds if they think the other people are of the right social status—which in Woodford usually just means being white-collar too. Working-class people are not welcomed so freely in clubs, pubs or in the district at all, as is evident from what middle-class residents, the older ones in particular, said about recent changes in the local population. A recurrent complaint of the suburb-dweller, as we remarked in Chapter I, is that the place is not what it was. We were told this time and again in Woodford.

> 'All sorts of people have come into Woodford since the war who ought never to have come into it, if you know what I mean. There's not such a good class of person here as there used to be.'
>
> 'It's bringing the Central line out here that's made all the difference. You get a different class of person here from what you used to get before the war.'
>
> 'The working class have moved into the district more and more. The class has definitely gone down.'

Manual workers, for their part, were perfectly well aware of this resentment, and reacted in kind.

> 'In Woodford they haven't got much, but they're what I class as jumped-up snobs. They think they're better than what you are.'
>
> 'They try to be what they can't around here. They've never had it and they're just jumped up and they think they're just it.'
>
> 'The middle-class people here are snobs. They put on airs and graces. They are all out for show—nothing in their stomachs but nice suits on.'
>
> 'Some people here are more classy—or they try to be. They're just the same as we are, but they try to be something different.'

If middle-class people say that the working class 'lowers the tone' of the area, the working-class reply that the middle class are snobbish and aloof, claiming a superior status to which they are not entitled.

Enclaves of class

The antagonism is at its most sharp when people from the

two classes are close to each other. In the main, the working class in Woodford live in recognizably working-class 'enclaves'—parts of South Woodford, for instance, or a network of roads just north of Wanstead High Street, or the Council estates. As a man living near Woodford Green put it, 'The less fortunate people—I prefer to call them that rather than the working class—the less fortunate people don't live in this part of Woodford. They tend to be combined in particular areas, and I must say they seem to get on with each other very well.'

People were well aware of the class character of different districts. 'The working class live on the other side of Well Road', said Mr. Burgess, 'but not this side.' 'You wouldn't get', Mr. Long told us, 'the Crescent and Albin Park mixing with Franklin Road and Arkwright Road.' The distinction between the two districts on opposite sides of the railway is particularly sharp. Mr. Day explained, 'The railway line is the dividing line—those who live below are not thought of as being as high class as those who live above.' 'You wouldn't expect', said Mr. Scott, 'the people here to go hobnobbing with the people on the Council estate on the other side of the line.' 'I'm no snob', another man asserted, 'but it seems to me it's south of the railway line you've got the working classes in Woodford.'

We plotted the addresses of our informants on a map of the borough and then distinguished the working-class people living in 'clusters'—that is, amongst other manual worker informants—and those who were living amongst middle-class informants. Of the 355 working-class people in the general sample, 79% lived in clusters, in 'working-class districts'. These people were certainly aware of the local middle class. They see them in the shops—'They expect to be served before you just because they've got money.' They meet them as they walk about the borough—'If you take a walk up Greenacres Estate, they look at you and say, "Oh, look at all those children".'

But it is the manual workers living in middle-class areas

who complain most strongly about the snobbishness of their neighbours. Very few people of any kind in Woodford were prepared to go to the lengths of saying all their neighbours were 'stand-offish'. But working-class people were much more inclined to do so if they lived in middle-class roads— only 6% of the 282 working-class people who were living in working-class 'clusters' said neighbours were stand-offish, against 19% of the 73 who were not. When the middle-class people told us what they thought of having working-class people as neighbours, we could see why.

> 'It's not like Cromer Gardens used to be with all these East Enders in the road. The noise and the ice-cream papers and the wireless on all day.'

So upset were one retired couple at the working-class people who had moved alongside them that they had decided to move right away, to the south coast.

> 'On both sides they're recent, and on both sides from the East End. That's what has really made us decide to retire to Worthing. You can't talk to those people, we just don't speak the same language. Some of the old residents down the road asked me who was coming here after us. We've sold the house to a young architect and his wife, so we were able to assure them that *we* hadn't let them down.'

Those who stayed did not attempt to make friends of the intruders.

> 'Those people from the East End are good-hearted folk, but you couldn't make friends of them. Sounds a bit snobbish, I know, but we've got nothing in common with them.'

A gardener living in a middle-class road saw it from the opposite point of view. 'I only know two people in this turning', he said, 'We've been here twelve years, but we don't seem to have got to know people.' 'It's very difficult', said a docker from Poplar, also in a middle-class district, 'We've been here for six years and we haven't really made any friends at all.' Others similarly placed complained about the aloofness of their neighbours. The wife of a retired lorry-driver said: 'People round here look down on you. At the other end of this road they're people more like myself. But round there they are *very* snobbish.' The widow of a porter said, 'They're snooty round here. I get the impression they don't think we're good enough to live here.'

Still two classes

Objective differences in Woodford are slighter than they have ever been in the past. Not only have incomes come closer together, but (despite middle-class protests to the contrary) people in different classes also spend their money on the same kinds of things, on cars, on refrigerators, on washing machines. The two classes live in the same kind of district, often in the same kind of houses, and have much the same kind of hopes for their children. One can see what Hoggart meant when he talked about 'our emerging classlessness'.[1]

And yet these are only the outward and visible signs of class. Inside people's minds, as we have shown in this chapter, the boundaries of class are still closely drawn. Classlessness is not emerging there. On the contrary, the nearer the classes are drawn by the objective facts of income, style of life and housing, the more are middle-class people liable to pull them apart by exaggerating the differences subjectively regarded. In Woodford this has been done with such success that to a very large extent social relationships are confined to one side or another of the dividing line in the mind. In many ways Woodford is a friendly place; its inhabitants have an active social life. But this friendliness is bounded by class lines. If middle-class people have friends they are usually middle-class too; if working-class people have friends they are usually working-class too. There were still two Woodfords in 1959, and few meeting-points between them.

[1] Hoggart, R., 'Speaking to Each Other', p. 135.

XI

IN CONCLUSION—LIFE IN A SUBURB

IN one important way, Woodford has turned out to be much as we expected. Kinship ties there are much looser than in Bethnal Green. When a couple marry they set up a genuinely independent household; relatives' homes are more often connected by occasional missions, not by the continuous back and forth which make two homes into one in Bethnal Green. Kinship matters less—friendship more. That is no surprise. But we also asked other questions, whose answers were not as we expected. This applies particularly to four important points—old age, the feminine core to the kinship system, the friendliness of the suburb and the difference between the working classes of the two districts.

1. Old age. Money apart, Bethnal Green could almost have been designed expressly for aged parents, so well is it suited to their needs, providing them with company, care, and, at least if they are mothers, a place of eminence in the family. How could Woodford reach such a standard? Was it not inevitable that more independence for the young would mean less security for the old? It sounds plausible, but it is not true, not wholly so at any rate. As we showed in Chapter IV, the generations do come together, but not so much on marriage as on bereavement. Bethnal Green daughters give up adolescent freedoms and return to their mother's hearth when they marry; Woodford parents come to their children's door when one of them is left widowed or when both are too old or too infirm to take care of themselves any longer. From a purely physical point of view, Woodford seems to look after its old as well as Bethnal Green.

This is not to say there is nothing to worry about. Physical care is only one of the needs of old age. Others are not so well satisfied in Woodford—the need for respect, the need to give as well as receive, the independence which is necessary to a sense of identity. To some extent this is inevitable. Woodford belongs more fully to a modern technological world than does Bethnal Green, and is therefore less in awe of tradition. Woodford wives do not pay great heed to their mothers' opinions about baby-care, as they do in Bethnal Green; they are more likely to consult the clinic, their doctor or each other. The wisdom of age is not valued in the same way. The generations have been apart for many years and, this being so, they are almost bound to have grown apart too. It may be a shock to both sides when they reunite, and find each other so prickly.

But if the friction of which we saw evidence is partly unavoidable, it is not wholly so. A good deal of the trouble arises because the generations so often have to live under the same roof. Here Woodford is at a disadvantage compared with Bethnal Green. The latter has more variety of accommodation, one- and two-room flats and floors, tiny houses as well as large, and Mums can use their influence with rent-collectors to get suitable quarters for each segment of their family. The old can live in their own little place across the road from their daughter. But things change as one goes towards the periphery of the city—at the centre there are more small dwellings in large buildings, flats and old houses, and in the suburbs more large dwellings in small houses. In Woodford the housing is as nearly uniform as the most hide-bound municipal estate—it has almost nothing but three- or four-bedroom houses for families with children, ill-designed for the elderly. The generations move in together because they have no alternative—there is no suitable accommodation nearby.

In the long run more small houses will presumably be

built, mixed up with the larger, so that whole families can more often live *near* to each other. There is scope for a private counterpart to the Council dwellings which are becoming increasingly popular with the old. Meanwhile, most people will have to make do as best they can in houses not designed with the needs of three generations in mind. It seemed to us that wherever a semblance of a separate dwelling for the old had been carved out inside the house, a cooking-stove and a wash-basin installed, or best of all a separate bathroom and kitchen, the aged were more content because they enjoyed more independence and suffered less wound to their pride. The younger people benefited through being on their own too, for at least some of the time. What can be done depends upon the size and layout of the house, and how many people have to fit into it. But some sort of physical conversion should often be possible and worthwhile. It is now obligatory, under the House Purchase and Housing Act of 1959, for local authorities to make grants for conversions and improvements. This could be a most useful measure for old people. But perhaps Councils could, in co-operation with voluntary bodies, do something more—not just to publicize the existence of this new Act (which is probably unknown to almost all the citizens of Woodford, as of everywhere else), but to provide a source of architectural advice. The husbands of Woodford, as we noticed in Chapter II, are many of them formidable handymen already. But this does not mean they would be averse to suggestions made on the spot by a knowledgeable person about ways of reorganizing rooms, plumbing and heating to suit the needs of old people without impairing the eventual value of the house. This new architectural service would naturally draw together what is already known—and it is considerable—about the special housing needs of old people. Where a local authority was already building bungalows for them it would be particularly easy to add on the additional function of advising private owners and landlords about conversions and adaptations.

There is another service which would be especially helpful

to the young. One of our informants was an aged woman who had recently spent six weeks in the nearby Langthorne Hospital so that her children could have an urgently needed break. She was exceptional. Far more help of this sort is needed. Langthorne Hospital has been a pioneer in providing for temporary admissions of aged patients in order to relieve their relatives.[1] Sheldon[2] suggested short-stay hostels to help meet the same objective; other measures include the fuller use of day hospitals and home helps. Relief of this sort not only helps hard-pressed relatives; by assisting old people to stay well, it also eases the pressure of demand for beds in chronic wards.

The social services generally can do much to relieve the financial pressure on old people. They can usually manage at the moment, without being an intolerable burden on the younger generation, because they have some support from their pension. This is not to say it is adequate. In Chapter VI we saw how much the income of manual workers falls upon retirement, and how much scope there is for an improved pension which would do a little more to maintain their standard of living in old age. There is another vital job for the social services, State and voluntary, and that is to care for the large minority of people who have no families to aid them. We referred to the size of this minority in Chapter V, and we would say that the task of supporting them adequately has only been started. The kind of old people who were isolated in Woodford needed more frequent visits from somebody—a few of them saw practically nobody. They also needed more help with housing, small old people's homes with a family atmosphere about them, 'foster children' and, generally, the sense that society had not deserted them.

2. Mothers and daughters. In the light of our research in Bethnal Green, and that in other working-class districts of Britain, we ventured to expect 'the stressing of the mother-daughter tie to be a widespread, perhaps universal, pheno-

[1] DeLargy, J., 'Six Weeks In: Six Weeks Out'.
[2] Sheldon, J. H., *The Social Medicine of Old Age,* pp. 197–8.

menon in the urban areas of all industrial countries'. But we went on to qualify this statement by saying 'at any rate in the families of manual workers'.[1] Manual workers seemed to have more need for the extended family as the 'woman's trade union'. Working-class mothers suffered more from insecurity. They received uncertain and ungenerous house-keeping allowances even when their husbands were not out of a job. Death rates were high, and if husbands were not killed in war or in peace, they were always liable to desert. Woman's only protection, we argued, was herself. The wife clung to the family into which she was born, and particularly to her mother.

Since middle-class wives were not beset by such insecurity we did not expect them to be so dependent on their own families of origin. We imagined that the closeness of husband and wife (of which we saw some sign in Chapter II) might exclude any special bond between a wife and her mother. We were not completely wrong—the mother-daughter tie is not so tight as in Bethnal Green. But it is there all the same; the feminine relationship is still stressed; it is very often still the axis of such extended family relationships as there are. We gathered together the evidence for this in Chapter VI, and in Chapter VII we saw that occupational mobility did not seem to set up barriers between mothers and daughters as it did between fathers and sons. Insecurity or not, married women have a common interest in children and housekeeping, in their common occupation, which is stronger than the interest shared by fathers and sons engaged in quite different occupations.[2] We would now remove the qualification from the above statement.

3. *Friendliness.* Bethnal Green people were warm, easy-going, humorous and friendly—friendly to us and friendly to each other. We explained this overflowing spirit of community in two ways. Bethnal Greeners had lived in the district

---

[1] *Family and Kinship in East London,* p. 163.

[2] An as-yet-unpublished study by Michael Young and Hildred Geertz in a San Francisco suburb suggested that the same tie between mothers and daughters could be noticed there.

for a long time and therefore knew each other well. They also had the benefit of their localized extended families; each member was a link with yet further relatives, friends and neighbours. The explanation was made more cogent by the unfriendliness of people on the housing estate at Greenleigh, who had neither lived there a long time nor brought their relatives with them. We expected that Woodford would turn out to be another Greenleigh.

This has turned out not to be so. People in the suburb are on the whole friendly, neighbourly and helpful to each other. They attend clubs and churches together, they entertain friends and neighbours in their homes, they like (or at any rate they profess to like) their fellow-residents. All this does not make us think our explanation of Bethnal Green friendliness was wrong. Long residence and kinship were the clues there. But obviously this explanation will not do for Woodford since both of these two conditions are for the most part absent.

The explanation seems to be that many people, particularly middle-class people of the sort who live in Woodford, have a certain capacity or skill at 'making friends'. Bethnal Greeners do not need this capacity. Whether they make any effort or not, they have plenty of friends around them. They do not have to make friends, their friends are ready-made, as it were, and presumably this was why they were so lost when they were transported to the strange environment of the housing estate. Middle-class people may also be more adept at the task because they have the confidence which a sense of class superiority gives. In so far as this is true, and as they show it, the friendliness of the middle classes may be at the cost of antagonism *between* the classes. The working classes of Woodford are made to feel inferior in their mixed society in a way they are not in Bethnal Green, and it is this which is partly responsible for their less enviable lot in the suburb.

We do not say that 'friendliness' has the same character in the two districts. In Bethnal Green people took each other

128

very much for granted. In Woodford relations are not so easygoing. Standards are harsher. A newcomer to a street—and, of course, there are far more 'newcomers' in the suburb than in Bethnal Green—will not necessarily be accepted into a neighbourhood group. She has to show she is worthy of it, be the right sort of person, have a decently furnished home of her own, speak with the right accent, be neatly dressed, enjoy living in Woodford but not so much that she would greatly mind moving, have a readiness to engage in conversation, and, above all, be rather extroverted, able to march out and meet people without being too shy about it. Sociability becomes a sort of profession. To get on well, people have to some extent to put on a front of *bonhomie*, and maybe leave out some part of their personality in the process. They have to conform—in a typical Woodford avenue there seems more uniformity of gardens, attitudes and opinions than in an East End 'turning'. Maybe uniformity is one of the prices we have to pay for sociability in a more mobile society.

4. A different working class. The Woodford working class has proved even more different from the Bethnal Green than we had expected. As we see it now, looking backwards, the special quality of Bethnal Green depended, much more than we allowed for before we had made a comparison with another kind of district, upon the fact that it was a 'classless' or rather a one-class community. A vital question to ask about any stratified society (and that means all) is how members of the classes or groups regarded as being at the bottom manage to keep their self-respect. How do people in the 'lower classes' satisfy this vital psychological need? Bethnal Green provides one kind of answer; indeed its answer is in essentials probably the same as that of most communities in Britain, from mining villages to steel towns, which are inhabited almost exclusively by working-class people. Bethnal Greeners are, of course, well aware that people in other parts of London are much better off, and that many of them look down on manual workers of the kind who inhabit Bethnal Green—or the 'slums' as the borough would be (and is) called by its detractors. But the local people have succeeded in erecting two powerful defences against middle-class notions.

The first is their long-settled community. Because they have lived in it so long, most Bethnal Greeners are surrounded by scores of people they know intimately, people who are one minute relations, another minute neighbours, another minute friends, another minute Borough Councillors. The emphasis is not so much on the individual home, prized as this is, as on the informal collective life outside it in the extended family, the street, the pub and the open-air market. There is the sort of bantering warmth in public which is reserved in Woodford for the home. The dense texture of local life means that it is not easily penetrated by external influences. Just because it is internally so cohesive the local community is able to erect a wall against disturbing ideas from outside. The nature of the community also means that it is almost impossible to 'put on airs' or to claim any superiority just because you earn more or spend more than your neighbour. Your neighbour remembers you as a boy, and knows your aunt is no better than she should be, and will 'take you down a peg' if you become 'toffee-nosed'. The network of personal relationship acts as a check on the acquisitiveness of local people.

> 'They stand well with plenty of other people whether or not they have net curtains and a fine pram. Their credit with others does not depend on the subtleties of behaviour in their many face-to-face relationships. They have the security of belonging to a series of small and overlapping groups, and from their fellows they get the respect they need.'[1]

The second defence is the political system, which is based ideologically on some variant or another of the labour theory of value. In a study we made into attitudes to the grading of different occupations we found that a substantial minority of men put non-manual jobs at the bottom of the scale and

---

[1] *Family and Kinship in East London*, p. 134.

manual jobs at the top. Managers and the like were lowly placed because they did not actually make anything, while men who made things with their hands were regarded as much more important. Agricultural labourers were valued highly because 'you can't do without grub', and bricklayers because 'you've got to have food and after that you've got to have houses.'[1] Linked with this view of manual work is allegiance to trade unions and to a Labour Party whose purpose is (to quote the beginning of Clause 4 of its Constitution), 'To secure for the workers by hand or by brain the full fruits of their industry.' A close community, the extended family, informal and formal collective organization and socialism are all of a piece.

These two defences depend for their full effectiveness upon there being only one class in the community. In a district of mixed classes like Woodford, working-class people cannot for the most part preserve their self-respect by these means. They have available one other support which they share with the inhabitants of Bethnal Green and everywhere else. As citizens they have the same rights and duties—to fight, to vote, to criticize, to receive the benefits of the welfare state— as anyone else. What T. H. Marshall called the 'basic human equality of membership'[2] of the nation helps to reduce the harshness of inequalities, in Woodford as anywhere else. A working-class informant spoke to us about the virtues of England.

> 'I can sit here and scream about the Government. I can go to my dentist and have a tooth out without paying. I can walk down the road without getting knocked over the head. Yes, I'm very loyal to the old country.'

Here he was stressing his loyalty to a country in which he was just as much a citizen as the man with the biggest house on Monkham's Estate.

But in general the Woodford working-class have to contend with middle-class views which are a much greater, more

[1] Young, M., and Willmott, P., 'Social Grading by Manual Workers'.
[2] Marshall, T. H., *Citizenship and Social Class*, p. 9.

immediate challenge than they are in Bethnal Green. In face of the challenge, they divide, a part clinging rather unconvincingly to a version of the Bethnal Green code, a part accepting middle-class views and setting out to become middle-class themselves, in attitude, in house and furniture, and in politics.

This they can do without too much frustration because they live, alongside those who have already entered the middle class, in an expanding economy. Britain's national income has risen by a quarter in ten years and that helps to create new opportunities for advancement. Higher incomes mean that class divisions are no longer so securely based upon the structure of workplace; the new divisions are based more upon consumption standards. Middle-class Woodford was in tune with the times when it blamed the working classes not so much because they did manual work as because they did not know how to spend their money. But in fact all classes in Woodford are more and more striving to earn more and spend it on the same things, in and around the home and the little car that goes with it. Most people seem contented enough with the result. They are proud of the place, or at any rate of the little province within it where husband and wife exercise their joint dominion.

> 'I often feel at the end of the day that all my efforts have been of no avail. I remember all the polishing and cleaning, washing and ironing, that will have to be done all over again, and like many other housewives I wish that my life could be a bit more exciting sometimes. But when the evening fire glows, when the house becomes a home, then it seems to me that this is perhaps the path to true happiness.'

Thus spoke one of our Woodford diarists. She could not be accused of a dangerous dissatisfaction.

APPENDIX 1

Methods of Sampling

As explained in the Introduction, the three main samples in this inquiry were as follows:

1. *The old age sample*—a sample of 210 people of 'pensionable age' or over (65 for men, 60 for women) drawn from the records of six doctors' practices in the Borough of Wanstead and Woodford.

2. *The general sample*—a random sample of 939 people, drawn from the electoral register, of the adult population in the Borough of Wanstead and Woodford.

3. *The marriage sample*—a sub-sample, drawn from the general sample, of parents with at least two children under 15.

The methods of sampling and the representativeness of the samples are now discussed for each in turn.

The old age sample

The method used to draw this sample was the same as that used by Townsend in Bethnal Green, with one exception. Instead of taking an initial sample from doctors' practices in Woodford, we approached the six general practitioners who were members of the College of General Practitioners.[1] Had the six practices in which these members worked seemed to be very different from the other twenty-two practices in Woodford, we could not have proceeded in this way, but as far as we could judge they were not. The six practices were geographically scattered throughout the district, so that a sample drawn from them was likely to include people from all parts of Wanstead and Woodford. And officials of the Essex Executive Council of the National Health Service whom we consulted told us that the practices were 'fairly representative of Health Service practices in the area', a view which seemed to be

[1] We are grateful to the Research Committee of the College for their help.

confirmed when we compared the age of the doctors selected and the size of their practices with those in the borough generally.[1] All the doctors approached agreed to co-operate.

The method used for selecting names and addresses was as follows. In the records of each practice, we drew every fourth card, and, if the person whose name was drawn was of pensionable age or if the age was not shown, the name and address went into the initial sample. This method produced an initial list of 664 names and addresses from the six practices. From these we drew, in stages and at random, the numbers we found we needed to produce a final sample of about 200 people interviewed. By the end, we had actually drawn a total of 323 names from the initial list. Sixteen of these were eliminated at the outset, because when called on they proved to be below pensionable age. The result of visits made to the remaining 307 addresses is shown in Table XX

TABLE XX

RESPONSE IN OLD AGE SURVEY

Names drawn	307
Not contacted (death, removal, etc.)	47
	—
Number contacted	260
Refusals	50
	—
Number interviewed	210
	—

The refusal rate—19% of people contacted—is high for a survey of this kind.

The sample interviewed is compared with the Census[2] in Tables XXI, XXII, and XXIII; it should be remembered that the aged population of the borough may have changed between 1951 and 1957, when the old age sample was interviewed.

[1] We are grateful to the N.H.S. Executive Council for Essex for their advice and for providing statistical information.
[2] Census 1951, *County Report—Essex.*

TABLE XXI
SEX OF OLD PEOPLE IN WANSTEAD AND WOODFORD

	Census	Old Age Sample
Men	30%	29%
Women	70%	71%
Total %	100%	100%
Number	9,270	210

TABLE XXII
MARITAL STATUS OF OLD PEOPLE IN WANSTEAD AND WOODFORD

	Males		Females	
	Census	Old Age Sample	Census	Old Age Sample
Single	6%	5%	19%	15%
Married ..	72%	79%	40%	32%
Widowed and divorced ..	22%	16%	41%	53%
Total % ..	100%	100%	100%	100%
Number ..	2,778	61	6,492	149

TABLE XXIII
AGE OF OLD PEOPLE IN WANSTEAD AND WOODFORD

	Males		Females	
	Census	Old Age Sample	Census	Old Age Sample
60–64	—	—	} 54%	44%
65–69	39%	34%		
70–79	49%	56%	34%	37%
80 and over ..	12%	10%	12%	19%
Total % ..	100%	100%	100%	100%
Number ..	2,778	61	6,492	149

The main differences are that the old age sample includes more women over 80 than the Census and less under 70; it also has a larger proportion of widows and a smaller proportion of spinsters and married women.

Selection of general sample

The Electoral Register, published in February 1959, from information collected in October 1958, contained 45,225 names. We drew out 1,190 names and addresses. The response is shown in Table XXIV.

TABLE XXIV

RESPONSE IN GENERAL SURVEY

Names drawn	1,190
Living in 'non-private' household (e.g. hospital, school, nursing home) ..	14
Sample living in private households ..	1,176
Not contacted (death, removal, etc.) ..	129
Number contacted	1,047
Refusals	108
Number interviewed	939

The refusal rate, though not as high as for the old age sample, was 108 out of the 1,047 people contacted—just over 10%, nearly twice the rate in Bethnal Green.

Again comparisons with the Census can give some indication of the representativeness of the sample, though the previous warning should be borne in mind—Woodford's population may well have changed in important ways from 1951 to 1959. Tables XXV, XXVI, XXVII, XXVIII, provide the comparisons.

TABLE XXV

OCCUPATIONAL CLASS IN WANSTEAD AND WOODFORD
(Males only[1])

	Census	General Sample
I	8%	16%
II	29%	31%
III	50%	43%
IV	7%	5%
V	6%	5%
Total %	100%	100%
Number ..	20,395	464

TABLE XXVI

SEX OF ADULTS IN WANSTEAD AND WOODFORD

	Census	General Sample
Men	44%	49%
Women	56%	51%
Total %	100%	100%
Number ..	45,820	939

TABLE XXVII

MARITAL STATUS OF ADULTS IN WANSTEAD AND WOODFORD

	Males		Females	
	Census	General Sample	Census	General Sample
Married	78%	83%	63%	71%
Single	17%	14%	23%	16%
Widowed and divorced	5%	3%	14%	13%
Total %	100%	100%	100%	100%
Number ..	20,206	464	25,614	475

[1] 15 and over in Census. The Census also excludes some retired men whose occupations were not recorded.

Table XXVIII

Age of Adults in Wanstead and Woodford

	Males		Females	
	Census	*General Sample*	*Census*	*General Sample*
20–29	17%	14%	16%	11%
30–39	21%	23%	20%	21%
40–49	25%	23%	21%	22%
50–59	16%	24%	17%	21%
60–69	12%	9%	14%	14%
70–79	7%	6%	9%	9%
80 and over	2%	1%	3%	2%
Total %	100%	100%	100%	100%
Number ..	20,206	464	25,614	475

In the main there are only slight variations. One exception is the relatively high proportion of people in the general sample in the Registrar General's Social Class I. Another difference is that the general sample has a rather smaller proportion of women.

The marriage sample

The general sample included 162 married subjects who were living at home with their spouse and had two or more children under 15. From these we selected 50 at random for further, more intensive interviewing. The reason for selecting people at this stage of life was that we had done so in previous inquiries in Bethnal Green and at Greenleigh.

Two of the 50 people selected proved to have moved out of the borough between the first (general survey) interview and our re-call. A further four refused, leaving 44 who were interviewed. Of these, 23 were men and 21 women; in 15 interviews the spouse was present for at least part of the time. A majority—27—were in their 30s, four being in their late 20s and 13 in their 40s. Twenty-four had only two children, 11 had three, and nine had four or more.

APPENDIX 2

Interviewers' Instructions and Interview Schedule for General Survey

Notes and Instructions for Interviewers

1. *The Institute*

   The Institute of Community Studies is an independent research institute whose work is financed by philanthropic trusts. Since the Institute was started in 1954, we have published three books dealing with life in the East End of London —one on housing, one on the care of old people, and one on the problems of widows. But these enquiries were limited by being in a predominantly 'working-class' area, and an obvious next step was to investigate a 'middle-class' district. The area we chose was the suburb of Woodford.

2. *Earlier Research in Woodford*

   We began our study of Woodford (actually the Borough of Wanstead and Woodford) about eighteen months ago. The main idea was to see in what ways a suburb like this was different from the East End, and we decided at the outset to concentrate on the old people and find out how their needs differed in this contrasted district. We interviewed a small sample of old people and the main results of this research were given in a lecture at the British Association's meeting last year. Since this was written up in the local and national Press (and featured in *Tonight* on B.B.C. Television), some local people will have heard about it. The main finding of these interviews was that on the whole the old people in this district were being cared for and supported by children and other relatives, often going to live with their married children when they were widowed or infirm. One of the things that came out also was

139

that the kind of work the children did seemed to affect whether they lived near and saw much of the aged parents, which is one reason why in the present survey we are asking about the occupations of the children and other relatives.

3. *The Present Survey*

We are now extending the study for two reasons—the larger survey will give us bigger numbers, so that we shall be able to test some of the ideas suggested by the earlier interviews, and it will produce a much fuller picture of life in this district than we could get from the interviews with old people alone. If all goes well, we shall probably complete the picture by selecting a small number of the younger people from those you have interviewed to call back on and re-interview at greater length. We shall then have three sets of information to draw on in writing the final book—the general picture from the survey you are working on, and fuller interviews with both the old people and the young couples.

4. *How the Survey is Planned*

We have drawn at random a list of about one thousand names and addresses from the Electoral Registers for Wanstead and Woodford. The people drawn may be of any age over 20, men and women; some will be householders, others housewives, others the children or parents of the householder, others boarders or servants. Whatever their position in the household, the person whose name you are given is the person you must interview. The sample of names drawn is a representative cross-section of the adult population of the borough. We are collecting information only about people living in *private* households; the interview schedule would not be appropriate for other people. So if you find that the address listed is a school, nursing home, hostel or other type of institution, you should not proceed with the interview but should record this fact on the schedule. Note that this applies to staff as well as residents.

5. *Your Job*

The questions on the interview schedule are designed to provide precise information about the household and relatives of the person interviewed, and about how closely that person is connected to the neighbourhood through his work, pleasures and social life. The answers are to be recorded by ringing the appropriate code number of the schedule, or writing the answer in the space provided. When each interview has been checked and completed, the information will be transferred to a punched card for statistical analysis. This means that every question must be answered by selecting one of the answers allowed for on the schedule: any other answer would upset the way in which the statistics are to be worked out. If, however, for some reason or other *none* of the possible answers to a question seem to apply, please explain as clearly as possible on the schedule what the exact circumstances are. Also, where your informant does not know the answer, say about a brother or sister he has lost touch with, you will have to write D.K. (Doesn't know) in the appropriate space, instead of ringing any of the numbers.

6. *Survey Office*

Throughout the survey we shall be using an office in the district—at Snaresbrook House, where the Borough Council's Treasurer's department and the local W.V.S. are also accommodated. You should collect your interview forms and lists of names and addresses from this office and return them there. All queries on the interviewing should be raised at this office with the Field Supervisor. You will be asked to fill in a daily progress sheet, showing the work done, and you will normally be expected to return this with the completed interviews to the office either at the end of your day, or, if you are working late, before you start work the following day. On the daily progress sheet—and on the lists of names and addresses—you should record the calls made and show whether the people listed have been interviewed, or have refused, or have not been contacted. If you haven't been able to contact a person on your list you should make it plain whether a contact is possible, in which case you should show when this *can* be made (e.g. 'at work and will be in after 7 p.m.', or 'away on holiday and will be back after 20 May') or, if a contact is not possible, you should explain why (e.g. 'dead', 'no longer at this address', 'away in America for six months'). Incidentally, we are not following up people who have moved, even inside the district—the person listed should be interviewed only if he is still at the address on the list.

7. *Expenses*

Interviewers should record on their expenses sheet the time they have spent interviewing, their travelling time, and the cost of fares to and from Wanstead/Woodford and between addresses. We have not made any formal arrangements about breaks for meals, but interviewers working a full morning and afternoon, or an afternoon and evening will of course need a break for something to eat, and this need not be deducted from interviewing time. Forms should be returned to the survey office at Snaresbrook House on Thursday afternoon or Friday morning and payment will be made on Friday afternoon.

8. *Introducing Yourself*

The people to be interviewed will not know beforehand that you will be calling on them, so you will have to introduce yourself and explain what you want on the doorstep. A brief introduction is typed on the first page of the schedule. You will also have a postcard from the Institute, introducing you as one of our interviewers. You won't need to show this to everybody, just have it by you in case it is needed for identification. People sometimes ask 'Why me? Why not interview the people next door?' The answer is that we have drawn the names of a cross-section of Wanstead and Woodford residents by taking a random sample of names from the Electoral Registers and that it might put the results out to interview anybody else instead. Again, sometimes people are reluctant because, they say, 'I don't see the point of it. What good will it do?' It may do none: but we hope to publish a book on the results, which will be read by those interested in the social changes which are occurring in Britain. We know much less about the way we live as a nation than is often supposed. Lastly, some people need to be reassured that the information they give will not be passed on to neighbours, relatives, or officials. You can assure them that no one but yourself and the Institute's staff will see the completed questionnaires, and that their names will not be used in any way, and will not be published in any report of the inquiry.

9. *Refusals*

Of course, anyone is free to refuse an interview if they wish: if they are still reluctant to answer the questions after you have given them a thorough explanation of the purpose of the inquiry, it is best not to press them too hard. Simply write their name on the top first page of the schedule and 'refusal' in large letters. It very seldom happens that anyone who has agreed to be interviewed refuses to answer some of the questions when they are put to him: if anyone does so, do as much of the interview as you can, and write 'refuses to complete' on the first page. However, we have always found most people friendly and willing to co-operate without much persuasion. It is often a good idea to repeat a brief explanation of the purpose of the survey at the end of the interview, to make sure that there are no misunderstandings. You will also have a duplicated letter of thanks which you should give people before you leave.

10. *The Questions—Detailed Instructions*[1]

Table 1. *People in household and dwelling*

a) *Purpose of questions.* The idea is to record the following in Table 1:

(i) members of the subject's *household*, whether they are related or not;

(ii) relatives of the subject or of his/her spouse who live in the same *dwelling*, though not in the same household.

b) *Order of questions.* It is suggested that you ask first of all about the members of the household, putting the question at the head of Table 1, and fill in details for them. You should then check about boarders (people who eat in the subject's household, not lodgers—people who rent a room and cater for themselves) and check the number in the household. Then put question 2 and record in Table 1

---

[1] The interview schedule is reproduced on pp. 152-8.

the further relatives, if any, living in the dwelling but not the household. In the fifth column of the table, you will distinguish between those living in the same household, and those in the dwelling, but not the same household. The distinction must be kept in mind from the moment you put the first question (about the household), as some informants may need it to be explained to them.

c) *Household.* The definition is the group of people who all live in the same dwelling (including outbuildings which form part of the dwelling) and who are all catered for by the same person. In other words, people in the subject's household are people with whom he/she usually eats when at home.

d) *Dwelling.* A dwelling is a structurally separate dwelling and generally comprises any room or set of rooms having separate access to the street or to a common landing or staircase to which the public has access.

e) *Subject.* The subject is the person whose name is shown in the sample list and all relationships should be defined in relation to that person. The first horizontal column of the table is for particulars about the subject.

f) *Visitors.* Visitors should not be included, but people who usually live in the household (or dwelling) should be recorded if they are temporarily away from home, e.g. in hospital. 'Visitors' should, however, be included if they have been there for six months or more preceding the interview; people 'temporarily' away should be excluded if they have been away for six months or more preceding the interview.

g) *Relationship to subject.* It is important to record this accurately. For one thing, 'boy' or 'girl' won't do—you must put 'son' or 'daughter'. Be clear about the distinctions between parents and parents-in-law; people sometimes say that 'Mother' lives with them and you must make sure whether it is actually the *subject's mother* or his or her *mother-in-law*. Also, it is important to us to know whether a grandparent is the subject's mother's parent or father's parent: so if there is a grandparent in the dwelling *please* put 'M' or 'P' to distinguish—*e.g. for a maternal grandmother (mother's mother) put 'M grandmother' and for a father's mother put 'P grandmother'*.

h) *Sex.* Ring '1' for male, '2' for female.

i) *Age last birthday.* Do not simply ask for the age, since some people tend to answer by giving the age next birthday unless you are specific. If the age is not known exactly, put E for 'estimate' against the approximate age.

j) *Marital status.* 'Separated' people are counted as 'married' (code 1). In other words, if the spouse isn't living at home, we are not interested in whether this is because there has been a judicial separation or a quarrel, or because his or her job is the explanation.

k) *Working.* 'Full-time' work means thirty hours a week or more. 'Part-time' means twenty-nine hours a week or less, 'not working' means not gainfully employed at all outside the home. 'Outwork'—work done inside the home by women—is not counted as either full or part-time work. Those who are off work through strikes, illness etc. should be recorded according to their normal working hours. But those who have been off work through illness for twelve months or more should be treated as not working.

l) *Occupation.* We are asking about occupations right through the schedule, so it is important to get the rules about this clear at the outset. First, we are not so much interested in the person's job as a job, but as an indication of the kind of background the job gives him or her. This is why we say 'at 60 if over 60'—we know that some men change their job after about 60 for a less skilled or less responsible one. For instance, a skilled artisan might have to give up his job on health grounds and become a caretaker or a night-watchman while still working 'full-time', but we are really interested in the job he's done most of his life, not the one he happens to be doing now. With people over 60 who are still at work, you will probably find it easiest to say, 'What work are you doing?' and then, before you fill it in, 'Is that what you were doing at 60?' You would, of course, ask a retired person simply,

'What was your occupation at 60?' If people retired from full-time work before 60, then put down their occupation before retirement.

m) *Occupations of husbands.* Now for the second important point. We don't want to know the occupation of a married, widowed or divorced woman (including a woman separated from her husband); we want to know her *husband's* occupation (*even if he is now dead*). Single women are treated differently—you want their occupation (if they're over 60, then their occupation at 60 or at retirement if it was earlier). But for the other women the occupation recorded must be their husband's. (This applies *right through the schedule*: about a married, widowed or divorced sister or daughter, for instance, don't ask 'What is her occupation?' but 'What is/was her husband's occupation?'.) If both husband and wife are living in the dwelling (either the subject and his or her spouse, or a married pair of the subject's relatives) this will mean that you must have the same occupation for both. Whichever you put first in Table 1, husband or wife, write in the husband's occupation and then put 'ditto' for the spouse.

n) *Occupation—Alternatives.* All this means that you have the following alternatives in filling in the occupation column:

(i) You have an actual occupation listed. If the person is a man or a single or divorced woman it is that person's *own* occupation (at 60 if he or she is now over 60, at retirement if before 60). If a married or widowed woman, the husband's occupation (again at 60 etc.).

(ii) You have 'ditto'—for married men or women whose spouse has been listed above them in Table 1.

(iii) You have a dash '—' for a person who is unoccupied and always has been. This will, apart from children under five, only apply to a few people—a single woman who has spent all of her life looking after a relative, or a chronically sick man who has always been unable to work.

Never put 'housewife' or 'retired' (for obvious reasons)

or 'unemployed' (put the last occupation here). If the person is a child at school or a young man or woman at university or training college, put 'student' as their occupation.

o) *Accuracy of occupations.* You must try to get enough information to be fairly precise about the occupation (this again applies right through the schedule). For instance, 'manager' is too vague—is he a factory manager, sales manager, manager of a shop or a coffee-stall? 'Works in a factory' or 'Works at Jolliffe's' won't do either. Show whether the work is clerical or manual, skilled or unskilled, for an employer or not. Terms like 'engineer' are too vague also—it might mean designing bridges or working as a garage mechanic. With 'Civil Servants', ask for their grade—is it 'executive', 'administrative' or 'clerical'?

Question 2.   Other households in dwelling

As has been explained above, you should first fill in Table 1 for people in the household, ringing '5' in the column headed 'Same h'hold as sjt.'. After checking that you have completed the household, put question 2, and then, if you have ringed '1' and '3' under this question, go on to fill in a horizontal column for each *relative* living in the dwelling, this time ringing '6' in the 'same h'hold' column.

Questions 3 and 4.   Place of work and future in work

These questions must only be put to *subjects* who are working full or part-time, not to women subjects about their husbands.

Question 5.   Ownership or Tenancy

This is less complicated than it appears. In every case the subject's household will either own their house or flat (or be buying it), will rent it, or will have it rent-free (it goes with the job or someone has given them the free use of it). Secondly, either the subject or his/her spouse will own or rent it (or get it rent free) or someone else will (e.g. subject's father, sister, uncle, employer). So only one of the six possibilities will apply—only one number (from '1' to '6') can be ringed. In many cases, as when a married couple with young children live in a house on their own, you will not need to put question 5(b) at all.

Question 6.   Time in house

Either ring '1' (if subject born in the house) or fill in the year he/she *first* went to live in it.

Table 7.   Children

a) *Order.* The subject's children should be recorded in order from eldest to youngest. Ask first 'Who is your eldest child?' then 'Who comes next after Arthur?', or whoever it may be. Those who live in the same dwelling as the subject will already have been noted in Table 1, and should be left out here.

b) *Subject's children only.* We are concerned here only with the subject's own children. The husband or wife's children by a previous marriage should be left out, but the subject's own children by a previous marriage included. Step-children should therefore be left out, though any step-children who are in the *dwelling* will of course be recorded in Table 1. (This applies all through the schedule—we do not want information on page 3 about step-parents or step- or half-brothers or sisters, but if they are in the *dwelling* they will be recorded in Table 1.) We do not expect to get any information about illegitimate children, but if your informant refers to them spontaneously, record them with the other children and make a note that they are illegitimate. Any children legally adopted by the subject should be included. We are *not* concerned with children who have died.

c) *Whereabouts of children.* You should ask first 'Where does he/she live?' If it is clear from the answer that he does not live in Wanstead/Woodford, then write the district or town mentioned. For those living outside Greater London or Essex, it will be enough to give the county or city, or the country if abroad: e.g. Birmingham, Gloucestershire, South Wales, Australia—whatever the answer given may be. Within Greater London and Essex we want the borough or town: e.g. East

148

Ham, Greenwich, Chelmsford, Barking. If people give the name of a district which is only part of a borough, e.g. Hoxton or Seven Kings, then you may write that instead. If the answer is somewhere inside the borough of Wanstead and Woodford, then ask whether or not it is within five minutes' walk. The following places, in addition to 'Wanstead' and 'Woodford', are inside the borough and you should remember to check in these cases whether the child is within five minutes' walk—Aldersbrook, Snaresbrook, South Woodford, Woodford Green, Woodford Bridge, Woodford Wells, George Lane, Cambridge Park, Gates Corner.

d) *When last seen.* This means the last occasion on which they were met by the subject, even if only for a few minutes. Ring as follows:

Seen within last 24 hours   1
Seen over 24 hours ago but within a week .. 2
Seen over a week ago but within a month .. 3
Seen over a month ago but within a year .. 4
Seen over a year ago or never   5

e) *Child's occupation.* Remember that with married or widowed daughters you ask, 'What is/was her husband's occupation?' If people ask why you want to know about their children's occupations, explain that we think the kind of work the children (or their husbands) do may affect where they live; in particular, it may mean that they have to live farther away than they would like.

Table 8.   Parents

If the parents or parents-in-law live in the same dwelling, they will already have been recorded in Table 1, so leave the appropriate column blank. Leave out step-parents. If a parent is dead ring '2' in the first column and ask no more questions—with one important exception. If the father or father-in-law is dead but his wife is alive, and not already recorded as being in the dwelling, you *must* put in his occupation in the column headed 'Occupation'. When you are working across filling in her horizontal column, remember at the end that she, like all other women relatives in the survey, must be given her husband's occupation, so fill it in on *his* line. The rule is—

if *either* of the parents has a line filled in here, then the father's occupation *must* be recorded, and the same with parents-in-law.

Table 9. Father's occupation

This question has only to be asked when both the subject's parents are dead. If either of them is alive, we will have the information either in Table 1 or Table 8.

Table 10. Brothers and sisters

Leave out step- or half-brothers or sisters, and those living in the same dwelling. Again, you will find it easiest to list the brothers and sisters in age order. Ask first, 'Who is the eldest?' and 'Who is the next?' and so on. Remember we want the husbands' occupations for married and widowed sisters.

Questions 11 and 12. Relatives and friends visiting

These two questions are designed to allow us to compare how much relatives and non-relatives visit each other in Woodford. The questions are phrased to include 'popping-in' to borrow something or have a quick word, as well as social visits. But we are not concerned with social contacts *outside* the home. In question 12, we want to know about any non-relative whom the subject saw in the home (excluding, of course, professional callers like doctors or men from the electricity board). Remember the checks with both questions, they are put in because people often go wrong over these points.

Question 13. Social organizations

We are interested in any kind of social organization which holds regular meetings, whether for entertainment, education or voluntary work. Membership of a local Council should be included. We have included political parties because most local parties organize social functions, lectures, etc. We are not interested in membership of organizations like the Automobile Association, a loan or clothing club, or a trade union, which are mostly concerned with providing services for their members.

Question 16. Public house

People are sometimes a little self-conscious about their drinking habits. Reassure them, if you can, that we are not trying to find out who are the heavy drinkers, but only to discover how many find their entertainment locally.

Question 17. Birthplace

If the subject was born elsewhere than in the borough, write in the district, borough, town or country (as with relatives' whereabouts). Ask also, in these cases, when he/she *first* came to the borough, even if he/she has lived elsewhere for a while since.

Question 18. Education

Only ring '4' ('Yes') under the question about University if it really was a University (and include people still at University). Training colleges, technical colleges, etc. are not included. Under 'Which?' the answer should be 'London', 'Cambridge', 'Oxford', 'Manchester', etc.

Question 19. Household ownership

These should be ringed 'Yes' if *anybody* in the household has, or is paying for, the television, telephone, car. Include television sets on rental and cars owned by a firm but at the sole disposal of the person in the household.

Question 20. Social Class

This may seem odd, but we want people to do two things:
    (i) say what class they think they belong to, without giving them a choice; and
    (ii) say what they think, when given five specific classes to choose from.

Question 21. Opinions of others

This question must be put exactly in the form in which it is written. Don't be too easily put off if people say they don't know or can't say—add the prompt that we mean 'speaking *generally*'.

You will have a duplicated letter to leave with informants at the end of the interview, as you thank them for their help. Fill in the information on the right-hand side of page 5 immediately *after* the interview, but not in the informant's presence. You will see there is a space for comments on the interview: it may help us in calling back later if you put remarks like: 'Very co-operative', 'Helpful', 'Awkward', 'Friendly', etc.

INTERVIEW SCHEDULE FOR WANSTEAD/WOODFORD SURVEY

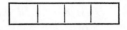

Introduction: I come from a social research organization called the Institute of Community Studies. You may have seen something about it in the local papers—we are doing a survey of Wanstead and Woodford, calling on a cross-section of people in the borough, and your name has come up. The idea is to help in writing a book about this district; we want to find out about housing and see how many members of each family live in the same house or in the district. Can I ask you a few questions—it won't take long? Anything you tell us will of course be treated as confidential—your name will not be published or used at all.

Table 1. First of all, can you tell me who lives in your household?

	Relationship to Subject	Sex M. F.	Age last birthday	Marital Status M. S. W. D.			Same h'hold as sjt. Yes No	Working Full- Part- Not time time		Occupation (at 60 if over 60; husband's occupation for married or widowed women)	
1	Subject	1 2		1 2 3 4				7 8 9			
2		1 2		1 2 3 4			5 6	7 8 9			
3		1 2		1 2 3 4			5 6	7 8 9			
4		1 2		1 2 3 4			5 6	7 8 9			
5		1 2		1 2 3 4			5 6	7 8 9			
6		1 2		1 2 3 4			5 6	7 8 9			
7		1 2		1 2 3 4			5 6	7 8 9			
8		1 2		1 2 3 4			5 6	7 8 9			
9		1 2		1 2 3 4			5 6	7 8 9			
10		1 2		1 2 3 4			5 6	7 8 9			

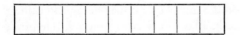

CHECK: Are there any boarders?
So there are........of you altogether?

2. Are there any other households living in this dwelling?

                        Yes   1
                        No   2

   IF YES (1) Are any of the people related to you or your husband/wife?

                        Yes   3
                        No   4

   IF YES (3) Who are they?

                   RECORD IN TABLE 1

IF SUBJECT IS WORKING FULL OR PART-TIME:

3. Can you tell me where you work (borough, district or town)?
   (WRITE IN) ....

4. And can you tell me whether you expect to continue in the same kind of job?

                        Yes   1
                        No   2

   Other (WRITE IN) ....

5. *a)* Are you (or any member of your household) renting this house/flat, or do you/they own it?

   b) Whose name is it (rent-book or house) in?

	Sjt. or Spouse	*Other Person*
Rent	1	4
Own (or buying)	2	5
Other	3	6

6. How long have you lived in this house/flat?

                   Born here   1
                   Came in...........(YEAR)

Table 7.   Have you any children who don't live here?

(IF ASKED): We want to find out how far the kind of work the children do affects where they live.

	Sex M. F.	Age last birthday	Marital Status M. S. W. D.				Whereabouts Wanstead/ Elsewhere Woodford (Specify) 5 min. walk Borough			When last seen Last Over W+ M+ Υ+ 24 24 hrs. — M. — Υ. hrs. — W.					Occupation (at 60 if over 60: husband's occupation for married or widowed daughters)	
21	I 2		I	2	3	4	2	3		I	2	3	4	5		
22	I 2		I	2	3	4	2	3		I	2	3	4	5		
23	I 2		I	2	3	4	2	3		I	2	3	4	5		
24	I 2		I	2	3	4	2	3		I	2	3	4	5		
25	I 2		I	2	3	4	2	3		I	2	3	4	5		
26	I 2		I	2	3	4	2	3		I	2	3	4	5		
27	I 2		I	2	3	4	2	3		I	2	3	4	5		
28	I 2		I	2	3	4	2	3		I	2	3	4	5		
29	I 2		I	2	3	4	2	3		I	2	3	4	5		

CHECK: So you have .... children altogether?

Table 8.   Can I ask about your parents? (ASK ONLY ABOUT PARENTS NOT IN SAME HOUSE)

	Alive Dead	Age last birthday	Whereabouts Wanstead/ Elsewhere Woodford (Specify) 5 min. walk Borough			When last seen Last Over W+M+Υ+ 24 24 hrs. — M — Υ hrs. — W					Where seen Subs. Parent's Other home home			Occupation (at 60 if over 60)	
Subject's father	I 2		2	3		I	2	3	4	5	6	7	8		
Subject's mother	I 2		2	3		I	2	3	4	5	6	7	8	× × × ×	×
Spouse's father	I 2		2	3		I	2	3	4	5	6	7	8		
Spouse's mother	I 2		2	3		I	2	3	4	5	6	7	8	× × × ×	×

9.   IF BOTH SUBJECT'S PARENTS DEAD, what was your father's occupation (at 60)? (WRITE IN)   ....

Table 10. Now can you tell me about your brothers and sisters who are alive now? (ASK ONLY ABOUT THOSE NOT LIVING IN THE SAME HOUSE)

	Sex M. F.	*Age last birthday*	*Marital Status M. S. W. D.*	*Whereabouts Wanstead/ Elsewhere Woodford (Specify) 5 min. walk Borough*	*When last seen Last Over W+ M+ Y+ 24 24 hrs. —M —Y hrs. —W*	*Occupation (at 60 if over 60; husband's occupation for married or widowed sisters)*
41	1 2		1 2 3 4	2 3	1 2 3 4 5	
42	1 2		1 2 3 4	2 3	1 2 3 4 5	
43	1 2		1 2 3 4	2 3	1 2 3 4 5	
44	1 2		1 2 3 4	2 3	1 2 3 4 5	
45	1 2		1 2 3 4	2 3	1 2 3 4 5	
46	1 2		1 2 3 4	2 3	1 2 3 4 5	
47	1 2		1 2 3 4	2 3	1 2 3 4 5	
48	1 2		1 2 3 4	2 3	1 2 3 4 5	
49	1 2		1 2 3 4	2 3	1 2 3 4 5	

CHECK: So you have .... brothers, and .... sisters altogether?

11. Now can I just check up? When was the last time any relative visited you in this house/flat (that's including those we haven't mentioned so far as well as those we have)?

Last 24 hours   1

Over 24 hours—week   2

Over week—month   3

Over month—year   4

Over year ago or never   5

CHECK: That was the last relative here, was it?

12. And, leaving out relatives altogether, when was the last time any friend or neighbour last visited you in this house/flat?

Last 24 hours   1

Over 24 hours—week   2

Over week—month   3

Over month—year   4

Over year ago or never   5

CHECK: That person isn't a relative, is it?

13. Are you a member of any social club or organization? (PROMPT: sports club, political party, church club, British Legion, dramatic society, etc.)

Yes   X

No   5

IF YES (X) When did you last attend any meeting?

Within 7 days	1
Within 1 month	2
Longer than 1 month ago	3
Never	4

14. What is your religion?

C. of E.	1
R.C.	2
Non-Conformist	3
Jewish	4
None	5
Other (WRITE IN)	....

15. Do you ever go to church?

Yes	Y
No	4

IF YES (Y) When did you last go?

Within 7 days	1
Within 1 month	2
Longer than 1 month ago	3

16. Do you ever go to a public house or hotel bar?

Yes	Y
No	4

IF YES (Y) When did you last go?

Within 7 days	1
Within 1 month	2
Longer than 1 month ago	3

17. Where were you born?

Same house	1
Elsewhere Wanstead or Woodford	2
Elsewhere (WRITE IN)	....

IF NOT 1 or 2,

When did you first move to Wanstead and Woodford?
Year...........................

18. Can I ask what age you finished at school?

14 or under	1
15	2
16 or more	X

IF 16 OR MORE (X) Did you go on to a University?

No	3
Yes	4

IF YES (4) Which? ....

19. Does your household have a

	Television?	Telephone?	Car?
Yes	1	3	5
No	2	4	6

20. *a)* Can I just ask this? If you were asked what social class you belong to, what would you say? (WRITE IN) ....

  b) If you were asked to say which *out of these five classes* you belong to, what would you say then? (SHOW CARD)

Upper	1
Upper middle	2
Middle	3
Lower middle	4
Working	5
Still can't say	6
Refuse	7

21. Which of the following statements is nearest to your opinion of the people around here? (PROMPT: I mean speaking *generally*.)

I don't notice them much	1
They are very easy to get on with	2
They are inclined to be stand-offish	3
Can't say	4
Refuse	5

Thank you. I hope I have not taken up too much of your time, and I am very grateful for your help. (HAND INFORMANT LETTER).

Date of interview   /   /   /

Day of week ....

Informant was:

Alone   5

Spouse present   6

Children present   7

Other (adults)   8

Interviewer's Name ....

Comments on interview ....

....

....

Subject's Name   ....

    Address   ....

....

Checked....................

APPENDIX 3

EFFECTS OF SOCIAL MOBILITY

IN the book as a whole occupation is the main criterion of social class, and we have also used it here in examining the effects of moving from one class to another. Men and single women were classified according to their own occupation, married women and widows according to their husband's. People over 60 were classified according to their occupation at 60. We based our grouping of occupations into social classes upon that of the Registrar General, partly because this enabled us to compare our results with Census data, and partly because of the convenience of having a ready-made index classifying most known jobs into occupational groups.[1] But we did not follow exactly the same scheme because we wanted particularly to distinguish, as the Registrar General's five-fold classification does not, between manual and non-manual occupations. This meant differentiating between various occupational groups in the Registrar General's Class III. Throughout the book, 'non-manual' occupations are those in the Registrar General's Class I (Professional), and Class II (Intermediate) together with those in Class III (Skilled) who are also in the Registrar General's Socio-Economic Groups 6 ('Clerical workers') and 7 ('Shop assistants'). Group 6 comprises all clerical workers, except for 'costing, accounting and estimating clerks' who appear in Class II; Group 7, as well as all shop assistants and salesmen, includes commercial travellers, canvassers and insurance agents.[2] 'Manual' occupations are the rest of the Registrar General's Class III, together with Class IV (Partly skilled) and Class V (Unskilled).

There are a number of occupations which we have classified as 'manual' which might well have been regarded as 'non-manual'. Foremen are an obvious example. The difficulty about them is that,

---

[1] See *Classification of Occupations.*
[2] For further details see e.g. *Census 1951, Occupation Tables*, p. xi and Table 1.

while some are virtually administrators, others do manual work alongside those they are supervising. In preliminary analysis, we distinguished the thirty-four 'foremen, inspectors and supervisors' in the general sample; when they turned out to be, in all sorts of ways, more like manual than non-manual workers, we decided to include them with the former. Similarly, we examined people in a number of other occupations that could be regarded as 'non-manual'—policemen, telephonists, laboratory assistants. There turned out to be only fourteen people in these 'marginal occupations', and since they also, in the ways we could measure, were not markedly different from manual workers generally, they too were included in this category.

Our two-fold classification into 'manual' and 'non-manual' occupations, though serving well enough for most purposes, was not adequate on its own for analysing the effects of occupational mobility, which are discussed in general terms in Chapter VII. We would only have been able to observe the influence of changing from 'manual' to 'non-manual' (or vice versa), and not the influence of what might be significant movements within each of these two groups. A two-fold classification would, in other words, conceal such movements as the clerk's son becoming a teacher or a dentist, or a labourer's daughter marrying a foreman. So, in examining the influence of social mobility, we have also analysed the material by reference to a six-fold classification.[1] This six-fold division is again based upon the Registrar General's classification, the six 'classes' being his Class I, Class II, Class III Non-manual, Class III Manual, (the last two being distinguished in the way explained above), Class IV and Class V.

In the tables that follow, both methods of classification—the 'two-fold' and the 'six-fold'—have been used. Tables XXIX and XXX, which show the amount of occupational movement from generation to generation, provide an illustration: Table XXIX is concerned only with movement between manual and non-manual occupations (i.e., the 'two-fold' model), while Table XXX shows the amount of movement in terms of six classes (i.e. the 'six-fold' model). In both tables, the percentages in boxes are those in the same class as their father.

---

[1] We also tried in preliminary analysis various other groupings—into three, four, five, nine and eleven classes—but the two-fold and six-fold divisions seemed to us to be the most meaningful.

TABLE XXIX

SOCIAL MOBILITY IN WOODFORD—TWO-FOLD

(General sample—married people)

		Father's Social Class	
		Non-Manual	Manual
Informant's Social Class	Non-manual	80%	47%
	Manual	20%	53%
Total %		100%	100%
Number		420	501

TABLE XXX

SOCIAL MOBILITY IN WOODFORD—SIX-FOLD

(General sample—married people)

	Father's Social Class					
Informant's Social Class	I	II	III Non-Manual	III Manual	IV	V
I	34%	25%	15%	9%	8%	2%
II	35%	41%	38%	27%	19%	11%
III Non-manual	16%	12%	27%	16%	13%	11%
III Manual	14%	18%	15%	36%	40%	35%
IV	1%	2%	—	7%	11%	21%
V	—	2%	5%	5%	9%	20%
Total %	100%	100%	100%	100%	100%	100%
Number	79	261	80	369	78	54

Tables XXIX and XXX show that there is in Woodford a good deal of mobility between generations. It is notable that nearly half of the sons and daughters of manual workers, for instance, are themselves in the 'non-manual' group. There is certainly enough mobility for us to be able to undertake a statistical analysis of its effects upon family contacts.

Now to examine the effects of this movement. The tables that follow refer to married subjects (including widowed and divorced); the single are excluded because most single people with parents alive are living with them anyway, and their inclusion might confuse the main issue. Tables XXXI and XXXII show the effect of mobility—up, down, and up and down combined—upon married people's contacts with their fathers (irrespective of the sex of the subject) first with the two-fold, then the six-fold classification. Tables XXXIII and XXXIV do the same for contacts with mothers.

TABLE XXXI

SOCIAL MOBILITY AND CONTACTS WITH FATHER—TWO-FOLD

(General sample—231 married people with fathers alive)

	Informant's Social Class			
	Same as Father	*Lower than Father*	*Higher than Father*	*Higher or lower than Father*
	(1)	*(2)*	*(3)*	*(2+3)*
Father seen in previous 24 hrs.	25%	29%	24%	25%
Seen earlier in previous week	37%	13%	37%	30%
Not seen in previous week ..	38%	58%	39%	45%
Total % ..	100%	100%	100%	100%
Number ..	144	24	63	87

TABLE XXXII

SOCIAL MOBILITY AND CONTACTS WITH FATHER—SIX-FOLD

(General sample—231 married people with fathers alive)

	Informant's Social Class			
	Same as Father (*1*)	*Lower than Father* (*2*)	*Higher than Father* (*3*)	*Higher or lower than Father* (*2+3*)
Father seen in previous 24 hrs.	30%	24%	22%	22%
Seen earlier in previous week	40%	17%	38%	32%
Not seen in previous week	30%	59%	40%	46%
Total % ..	100%	100%	100%	100%
Number ..	76	46	109	155

The only statistically significant difference in Table XXXI is that people who have moved down in occupational class had seen less of their fathers in the previous week than those in the same class. The same applies to Table XXXII, though this table also suggests that movement upwards may affect contacts with fathers too.

Contacts with mothers, it appears, are not affected like those with fathers—there is no indication in Tables XXXIII or XXXIV that people in a lower (or higher) class than their mothers see less of them than those who have remained in the same class. Indeed, those in a lower class actually see rather more of their mothers. The next step is to see whether the sex of the informant, in addition to that of the parent, makes any difference, and this is done in Tables XXXV to XXXVIII. Here, because the numbers are small, and in order to avoid over-complicating the tables, those who have moved up and down are combined throughout.

TABLE XXXIII
SOCIAL MOBILITY AND CONTACTS WITH MOTHER—TWO-FOLD
(General sample—342 married people with mothers alive)

	Informant's Social Class			
	Same as Mother (*1*)	*Lower than Mother* (*2*)	*Higher than Mother* (*3*)	*Higher or lower than Mother* (*2+3*)
Mother seen in previous 24 hrs.	27%	50%	33%	37%
Seen earlier in previous week	34%	21%	33%	30%
Not seen in previous week ..	39%	29%	34%	33%
Total % ..	100%	100%	100%	100%
Number ..	223	28	91	119

TABLE XXXIV
SOCIAL MOBILITY AND CONTACTS WITH MOTHER—SIX-FOLD
(General sample—342 married people with mothers alive)

	Informant's Social Class			
	Same as Mother (*1*)	*Lower than Mother* (*2*)	*Higher than Mother* (*3*)	*Higher or lower than Mother* (*2+3*)
Mother seen in previous 24 hrs.	30%	35%	30%	31%
Seen earlier in previous week	37%	21%	34%	30%
Not seen in previous week ..	33%	44%	36%	39%
Total % ..	100%	100%	100%	100%
Number ..	121	63	158	221

TABLE XXXV

SOCIAL MOBILITY AND CONTACTS WITH FATHER, ACCORDING
TO SEX OF INFORMANT—TWO-FOLD

(General sample—231 married people with fathers alive)

	Men		*Women*	
	Same class as Father	*Higher or lower than Father*	*Same class as Father*	*Higher or lower than Father*
Father seen in previous 24 hrs.	22%	13%	30%	35%
Seen earlier in previous week	36%	26%	39%	33%
Not seen in previous week ..	42%	61%	31%	32%
Total % ..	100%	100%	100%	100%
Number ..	87	38	57	49

In Tables XXXV to XXXVIII, the only statistically significant
difference is that (in Table XXXVI) between men who (on a six-
fold scheme) are in a higher or lower class than their father and
those who are in the same class. Apart from this, the difference
closest to statistical significance ($P < .20$) is that between mobile and
non-mobile men in Table XXXV. Contacts of women with fathers
and of men and women with mothers are not significantly affected
by social mobility.

TABLE XXXVI
SOCIAL MOBILITY AND CONTACTS WITH FATHER, ACCORDING TO SEX OF INFORMANT—SIX-FOLD
(General sample—231 married people with fathers alive)

	Men		Women	
	Same class as Father	*Higher or lower than Father*	*Same class as Father*	*Higher or lower than Father*
Father seen in previous 24 hrs.	29%	13%	32%	32%
Seen earlier in previous week	37%	30%	43%	33%
Not seen in previous week ..	34%	57%	25%	35%
Total % ..	100%	100%	100%	100%
Number ..	49	76	28	78

The left-hand section of this table is reproduced in slightly different form, as Table XII in Chapter VII.

TABLE XXXVII
SOCIAL MOBILITY AND CONTACTS WITH MOTHER, ACCORDING TO SEX OF INFORMANT—TWO-FOLD
(General sample—342 married people with mothers alive)

	Men		Women	
	Same class as Mother	*Higher or lower than Mother*	*Same class as Mother*	*Higher or lower than Mother*
Mother seen in previous 24 hrs.	27%	23%	27%	45%
Seen earlier in previous week	34%	35%	35%	27%
Not seen in previous week ..	39%	42%	38%	28%
Total % ..	100%	100%	100%	100%
Number ..	128	43	95	76

Effects of Social Mobility

TABLE XXXVIII

SOCIAL MOBILITY AND CONTACTS WITH MOTHER, ACCORDING
TO SEX OF INFORMANT—SIX-FOLD

(General sample—342 married people with mothers alive)

	Men		Women	
	Same class as Mother	*Higher or lower than Mother*	*Same class as Mother*	*Higher or lower than Mother*
Mother seen in previous 24 hrs.	30%	23%	29%	37%
Seen earlier in previous week	36%	33%	40%	29%
Not seen in previous week ..	34%	44%	31%	34%
Total % ..	100%	100%	100%	100%
Number ..	73	98	48	123

What conclusions can be drawn from the complex series of tables in this appendix? Social mobility, it seems, does affect people's contacts with their parents, in the following ways:

1. Contacts with fathers are affected rather than with mothers.
2. Sons' contacts with fathers are affected rather than daughters'.

But we would like to add a vital qualification: the statistical evidence for these conclusions is slight, and before any generalizations can be safely made on the relationship between occupational mobility and even the limited aspect of family structure we are considering, a great deal of further research will have to be done.

APPENDIX 4

ADDITIONAL TABLES

In Chapters III, VI and VII, the reader is referred to additional tables which provide supporting evidence. They are given here, under the following headings: (1) kinship comparisons between Woodford and Bethnal Green; (2) kinship comparisons between middle and working class inside Woodford; (3) help from daughters; (4) link between sisters.

1. *Kinship in Woodford and Bethnal Green*

TABLE XXXIX

CONTACTS WITH FATHERS—WOODFORD AND BETHNAL GREEN
(General sample—married people with fathers alive)

	Woodford	Bethnal Green
Seen within previous 24 hrs. ..	25%	38%
Seen earlier in previous week ..	34%	32%
Not seen in previous week	41%	30%
Total%	100%	100%
Number	234	216

TABLE XL

RESIDENCE OF SIBLINGS—WOODFORD AND BETHNAL GREEN
(General samples—siblings of married subjects)

Sibling's Residence	Woodford	Bethnal Green
Within five minutes' walk ..	5%	17%
Elsewhere in the same borough ..	10%	12%
Outside the same borough ..	85%	71%
Total of siblings %	100%	100%
Number	2,089	2,698

TABLE XLI
CONTACTS WITH SIBLINGS—WOODFORD AND BETHNAL GREEN
(General samples—siblings of married subjects)

	Woodford	*Bethnal Green*
Seen within previous 24 hrs. ..	8%	12%
Seen earlier previous week ..	15%	23%
Not seen in previous week ..	77%	65%
Total %	100%	100%
Number	2,110	2,722

2. *Kinship and Social Class in Woodford*

TABLE XLII
CONTACTS WITH MOTHERS, ACCORDING TO SOCIAL CLASS OF INFORMANT
(General sample—married people with mothers alive)

	Middle Class	*Working Class*
Seen within previous 24 hrs. ..	28%	34%
Seen earlier previous week ..	34%	32%
Not seen in previous week ..	38%	34%
Total %	100%	100%
Number	212	134

(The differences in this table are not statistically significant.)

TABLE XLIII
CONTACTS WITH FATHERS, ACCORDING TO SOCIAL CLASS OF INFORMANT
(General sample—married people with fathers alive)

	Middle Class	*Working Class*
Seen within previous 24 hrs. ..	18%	34%
Seen earlier previous week ..	40%	24%
Not seen in previous week ..	42%	42%
Total %	100%	100%
Number	141	93

Table XLIV

Residence of Siblings, according to Social Class of Informant

(General sample—siblings of married subjects)

Sibling's Residence		Middle Class	Working Class
Within five minutes' walk	..	4%	7%
Elsewhere in same borough	..	7%	13%
Outside the same borough	..	89%	80%
Total of siblings %	.. ..	100%	100%
Number	.. .. ..	1,192	897

Table XLV

Contacts with Siblings, according to Social Class of Informant

(General sample—siblings of married subjects)

		Middle Class	Working Class
Seen within previous 24 hrs.	..	8%	7%
Seen earlier in previous week	..	13%	18%
Not seen in previous week	..	79%	75%
Total of siblings %	.. ..	100%	100%
Number	.. .. ..	1,202	903

3. *Help from daughters*

TABLE XLVI

MAIN RESPONSIBILITY FOR HOUSEHOLD TASKS

(Old age sample—210 old people)

Main responsibility undertaken by	Shopping	Cooking	Cleaning	Washing
Self or spouse only ..	57%	66%	47%	54%
Self or spouse and relative	12%	9%	21%	16%
Self or spouse and other person	4%	2%	8%	2%
Daughter	15%	13%	10%	14%
Other relative	7%	7%	4%	4%
Other person	5%	3%	10%	10%
Total %	100%	100%	100%	100%

4. *Link between sisters*

TABLE XLVII

CONTACTS WITH SIBLINGS, ACCORDING TO SEX OF INFORMANT AND OF SIBLING

(General sample—siblings of married people)

	Men		Women	
	Brothers	Sisters	Brothers	Sisters
Seen in previous 24 hrs.	8%	5%	6%	10%
Seen earlier in previous week	14%	14%	13%	20%
Not seen in previous week	78%	81%	81%	70%
Total of siblings % ..	100%	100%	100%	100%
Number	469	536	518	587

APPENDIX 5

Tests of Statistical Significance

We used three tests to establish the significance of the tables: the χ^2 test for showing the validity of the different distribution of a variable between two or more groups; the standard error for a difference in proportions; and the t test for differences between averages. These tests produce a result in the form of the probability that the differences shown, or greater ones, might appear in a sample, even though there were no difference in the whole population from which the sample was drawn. This probability is denoted by P; thus P $<$.05 means that there are less than five chances in a hundred that a difference as great as, or greater than, that shown exists in the sample where there is none in the population. This is the limit that we have usually adopted for including tables, and also for differences in averages or proportions mentioned in the text.

In some instances we have aggregated all the siblings of informants (examples are Tables XL and XLI). The resulting samples are what are known as 'cluster samples' i.e. they are made up of variable numbers of siblings clustered around each informant. Such samples are, strictly speaking, not susceptible to testing by the usual methods, though there is a special method for testing them. We tried this method out with some small cluster samples but found it so laborious and time-consuming that to have applied it to tables covering all the 2,000-odd siblings would have been impossibly lengthy and costly. In practice, therefore, what we have done is to apply the usual standard error or χ^2 tests. We have usually either required a higher level of significance (with a value for P smaller than .01) or cited tables on siblings only when they are consistent with other independent evidence.

Two further points about the tables. First, when totals vary between two tables which are apparently dealing with the same people this is because small numbers of people have sometimes had to be excluded because of incomplete information. Second, in a few tables in which, because of rounding, percentages would otherwise have added to 99% or 101% we have adjusted them so that they add to 100% in order to simplify presentation.

Table Page Numbers		Title of Table and Difference Tested	Test used	Value of P
I	29	*Proximity of Parents—Woodford and Bethnal Green.* Parents in Woodford live farther away from married children than parents in Bethnal Green.	χ^2	<.01
2	33	*Contacts with Mothers—Woodford and Bethnal Green.* Woodford married people see mothers less often than do Bethnal Green married people.	χ^2	<.01
3	37	*Proximity of Nearest Married Child to People of Pension Age in Woodford and Bethnal Green.* People of pension age in Woodford less often have nearest married child living within five minutes' walk than those in Bethnal Green.	S.E.	<.01
		People of pension age in Woodford more often have nearest married child elsewhere in the borough than those in Bethnal Green.	S.E.	<.01
4	39	*Proximity of Nearest Married Child to People below and above Pension Age, in Woodford and Bethnal Green.* In Woodford people above pension age have a married child close by more often than do people below pension age.	χ^2	<.01

Table Numbers	Page	Title of Table and Difference Tested	Test used	Value of P
5	40	*People of Different Ages Living with Married Children.* The older the parents the more often they live in the same dwelling as a married child.	χ^2	<.01
6	54	*Marital Status and Last Contact with a Sibling—People below and above Pension Age.* Single people see more of siblings than married, widowed and divorced, both above and below pensionable age.	χ^2	<.01
7	63	*Average Weekly Income of People Working and Retired from Full-time Work, according to Social Class.* Working-class people have smaller incomes than middle-class, both in work and in retirement.	t	<.01
9	69	*Proximity of Parents to Married Men and Women.* Daughters live in the same dwelling as parents more often than sons do.	S.E.	<.01
11	78	*Parents' Residence according to District and Social Class of Informant.* Working-class people in Woodford live nearer to their parents than do middle-class people.	χ^2	<.01
		Bethnal Green people live nearer to their parents than do working-class people in Woodford.	χ^2	<.01
12	83	*Contacts of Men with Fathers, according to Occupational Mobility of Informant.* Married men in a different class from their fathers see them less often than do those in the same class as their fathers.	χ^2	<.05

Table Numbers	Page	Title of Table and Difference Tested	Test used	Value of P
13	91	*Club Membership and Attendance according to Social Class.* Middle-class people belong to, and attend, clubs and organizations more than working-class.	χ^2	<.01
14	93	*Church Attendance according to Social Class.* Middle-class people attend church more often than working-class.	χ^2	<.01
15	96	*Attendance at Public House according to Social Class.* Middle-class people go to public houses more often than do working-class.	χ^2	<.01
16	107	*Friends Visiting, according to Age.* Friends visit less often as people get older.	χ^2	<.01
17	109	*Friends Visiting, according to Social Class.* Middle-class people are more often visited by friends and neighbours than working-class people.	χ^2	<.01
18	116	*Ownership according to Self-Ascribed Class.* Manual workers who describe themselves as 'middle-class' more often live in owner-occupied houses than other manual workers.	S.E.	<.01
		Manual workers who describe themselves as 'middle-class' more often have a car than other manual workers.	S.E.	<.01
		Manual workers who describe themselves as 'middle-class' more often have a telephone than other manual workers.	S.E.	<.01

Table Numbers	Page	Title of Table and Difference Tested	Test used	Value of P
19	116	*Attendance at Church and Club, according to Self-Ascribed Social Class.* Manual workers who describe themselves as 'middle-class' more often attend church than other manual workers.	S.E.	<.01
		Manual workers who describe themselves as 'middle-class' more often belong to clubs than other manual workers.	S.E.	<.01
31	162	*Social Mobility and Contacts with Father —Two-fold.* Married people in a lower class than their fathers see them less than do married people in the same class as their fathers.	χ^2	<.05
32	163	*Social Mobility and Contacts with Father —Six-fold.* Married people in a lower class than their fathers see them less than do married people in the same class as their fathers.	χ^2	<.01
36	166	*Social Mobility and Contacts with Father, according to Sex of Informant—Six-fold.* Married men in a different class from their fathers see them less often than do those in the same class as their fathers.	χ^2	<.05
39	168	*Contacts with Fathers—Woodford and Bethnal Green.* Married people in Woodford see their fathers less often than do those in Bethnal Green.	χ^2	<.01

Table Numbers	Page	Title of Table and Difference Tested	Test used	Value of P
40	168	*Residence of Siblings—Woodford and Bethnal Green.* Siblings of Woodford married subjects live farther away than do siblings of Bethnal Green married people.	χ^2	$<.01$
41	169	*Contacts with Siblings—Woodford and Bethnal Green.* Woodford married people see less of siblings than do Bethnal Green married people.	χ^2	$<.01$
43	169	*Contacts with Fathers, according to Social Class of Informant.* Working-class married people see more of their fathers than do middle-class.	χ^2	$<.01$
44	170	*Residence of Siblings, according to Social Class of Informant.* Working-class married people more often have siblings living near than do middle-class.	χ^2	$<.01$
45	170	*Contacts with Siblings, according to Social Class of Informant.* Working-class married people see more of siblings than do middle-class.	χ^2	$<.05$
47	171	*Contacts with Siblings, according to Sex of Informant and of Sibling.* Married women see their sisters more often than their brothers and more often than married men see either brothers or sisters.	χ^2	$<.01$

APPENDIX 6

LIST OF REFERENCES

ARENSBERG, C. M. and KIMBALL, S. T. *Family and Community in Ireland.* Cambridge, Mass. Harvard University Press. 1948.

BENDIX, R. and LIPSET, S. M. (eds.) *Class, Status and Power: A Reader in Social Stratification.* London, Routledge & Kegan Paul. 1954.

BOOTH, C. *Life and Labour of the People in London.* 17 Vols. London, Macmillan. 1902.

BOTTOMORE, T. 'Social Stratification in Voluntary Organization'. *See* GLASS, D. V. (ed.) *Social Mobility in Britain.*

BURGESS, E. W. and LOCKE, H. J. *The Family: From Institution to Companionship.* 2nd edition. New York, American Book Company. 1953.

BUXTON, E. N. *Epping Forest.* London, Stanford. 1898.

CARR-SAUNDERS, A. M., JONES, D. C. and MOSER, C. A. *Social Conditions in England and Wales.* London, Oxford University Press. 1958.

CAUTER, T. and DOWNHAM, J. S. *The Communication of Ideas.* London, Chatto & Windus. 1954.

DELARGY, J. 'Six Weeks In: Six Weeks Out'. *Lancet.* Vol. 1. 1957.

DENNIS, N., HENRIQUES, F. and SLAUGHTER, C. *Coal is Our Life.* London, Eyre & Spottiswoode. 1956.

DOUGLAS, J. W. B. and BLOMFIELD, J. M. *Children Under Five.* London, Allen & Unwin. 1958.

DUNLOP, I. and KIMBALL, F. 'The Gardens of Wanstead House, Essex'. *Country Life.* 28 July 1950.

FESTINGER, L., SCHACHTER, S. and BACK, K. *Social Pressures in Informal Groups.* New York, Harper. 1950.

FIRTH, R. (ed.) *Two Studies of Kinship in London.* London School of Economics. Monographs on Social Anthropology, No. 15. London, Athlone Press. 1956.

GLASS, D. V. (ed.) *Social Mobility in Britain.* London, Routledge & Kegan Paul. 1954.

GORER, G. *Exploring English Character.* London, Cresset Press. 1955.

HOGGART, R. 'Speaking to Each Other', MACKENZIE, N. (ed.) *Conviction*. London, MacGibbon & Kee. 1958.

KERR, M. *The People of Ship Street*. London, Routledge & Kegan Paul. 1958.

KUPER, L. *Living in Towns*. London, Cresset Press. 1953.

KUTNER, B., *et al. Five Hundred Over Sixty*. New York, Russell Sage Foundation. 1956.

LIPSET, S. M. and BENDIX, R. *Social Mobility in Industrial Society*. London, Heinemann. 1959.

MARRIS, P. *Widows and their Families*. London, Routledge & Kegan Paul. 1958.

MARSHALL, T. H. *Citizenship and Social Class*. Cambridge, University Press. 1950.

MARTIN, F. M. 'Some Subjective Aspects of Social Stratification'. *See* GLASS, D. V. (ed.) *Social Mobility in Britain*.

MAYHEW, H. *London Labour and the London Poor*. Vol. 1. London, Woodfall. 1851.

MOGEY, J. M. *Family and Neighbourhood*. London, Oxford University Press. 1956.

MOLONEY, J. C. *See* SENN, M. J. E. (ed.) *Symposium on the Healthy Personality*.

MORRIS, J. N. and HEADY, J. A. 'Social and Biological Factors in Infant Mortality'. *Lancet*. Vol. 1. 1955.

MORTIMER, P. *Daddy's gone A-Hunting*. London, Michael Joseph. 1958.

MUMFORD, L. *The Culture of Cities*. London, Secker & Warburg. 1946 edition.

NEWTON, M. P. and JEFFERY, J. R. *Internal Migration*. London, H.M.S.O. 1951.

OGBURN, W. F. and NIMKOFF, M. F. *A Handbook of Sociology*. London, Routledge & Kegan Paul. 1956 edition.

ORWELL. G. *Coming up for Air*. London, Secker & Warburg. 1959 edition.

ORWELL, G. *Homage to Catalonia*. London, Secker & Warburg. 1938.

OSBORN, F. J. Preface to HOWARD, E. *Garden Cities of Tomorrow*. London, Faber & Faber. 1946.

PARSONS, T. 'A Revised Analytical Approach to the Theory of Social Stratification'. *See* BENDIX, R. and LIPSET, S. M. (eds.) *Class Status and Power*.

QVIST, A. *Epping Forest*. London, Corporation of London. 1958.

REES, A. D. *Life in a Welsh Countryside*. Cardiff, University of Wales Press. 1951.

SCHNEIDER, D. M. and HOMANS, G. C. 'Kinship Terminology and the American Kinship System'. *American Anthropologist*. Vol. 59. No. 6. Part I. December 1955.

SENN, M. J. E. (ed.) *Symposium on the Healthy Personality*. New York, Josiah Macy Foundation. 1956.

SHELDON, J. H. *The Social Medicine of Old Age*. London, Oxford University Press. 1948.

SINCLAIR, R. *East London*. London, Robert Hale. 1950.

SMITH, H. L. 'Influx of Population'. *See* BOOTH, C. *Life and Labour of the People in London*. Vol. 3.

STENTON, D. M. *The English Woman in History*. London, Allen & Unwin. 1957.

TITMUSS, R. M. 'The Position of Women'. *Essays on 'The Welfare State'*. London, Allen & Unwin. 1958.

TOWNSEND, P. *The Family Life of Old People*. London, Routledge & Kegan Paul. 1957.

WELLS, H. G. *Ann Veronica*. London, Unwin. 1909.

WHYTE, W. H. *The Organization Man*. London, Cape. 1957.

WILLIAMS, W. M. *The Sociology of an English Village: Gosforth*. London, Routledge & Kegan Paul. 1956.

YOUNG, G. M. *Victorian England: Portrait of an Age*. London, Oxford University Press. 1936.

YOUNG, M. and WILLMOTT, P. 'Social Grading by Manual Workers'. *British Journal of Sociology*. Vol. VII, No. 4. December 1956.

YOUNG, M. and WILLMOTT, P. *Family and Kinship in East London*. London, Routledge & Kegan Paul. 1957.

Census 1951. County Report—Essex. London, H.M.S.O. 1954.

Census 1951. England and Wales. Occupation Tables. London, H.M.S.O. 1956.

Census 1951. Classification of Occupations. London, H.M.S.O. 1956.

London Travel Survey 1949. London Transport Executive. 1950.

Neighbourhood and Community. Social Research Series. Liverpool, University Press of Liverpool. 1954.

Social Implications of the 1947 Scottish Mental Survey. Scottish Council for Research in Education. London, University of London Press. 1953.

INDEX